BRUCE WEBER'S
★ INSIDE ★
PRO FOOTBALL
◇ 1988 ◇

SCHOLASTIC INC.
New York Toronto London Auckland Sydney

PHOTO CREDITS

Cover: Photo of Doug Williams/Focus on Sports. **2, 23, 54, 78:** San Francisco 49ers. **3, 5, 22, 68:** Minnesota Vikings. **4, 16, 56:** New York Giants. **6, 40:** Cincinnati Bengals. **7, 42:** Houston Oilers. **8, 12, 80:** Los Angeles Rams. **9, 11, 24, 28:** Indianapolis Colts. **10, 32:** Miami Dolphins. **13, 30, 84:** Buffalo Bills. **14, 18, 66:** Chicago Bears. **15, 60:** Philadelphia Eagles. **17, 44:** Seattle Seahawks. **19, 26:** New England Patriots. **20, 21, 36:** Cleveland Browns. **34:** New York Jets. **38:** Pittsburgh Steelers. **46:** Denver Broncos. **48:** Los Angeles Raiders. **50:** San Diego Chargers. **52:** Kansas City Chiefs. **58:** Washington Redskins. **62:** Dallas Cowboys. **64:** Phoenix Cardinals. **70:** Tampa Bay Buccaneers. **72:** Green Bay Packers. **74:** Detroit Lions. **76:** New Orleans Saints. **82:** Atlanta Falcons.

ISBN 0-590-41728-2

Copyright © 1988 by Scholastic Books, Inc.
All rights reserved. Published by Scholastic Inc.

12 11 10 9 8 7 6 5 4 3 2 1   8 9/8 0 1 2 3/9

Printed in the U.S.A.   01

First Scholastic printing, September 1988

CONTENTS

INTRODUCTION:
The Road to Miami

Parity. What a wonderful word. Sports leaders love to talk about it. As they see it, parity means competition. With parity, every team has a chance to win. In the old days, NFL leaders loved to say, "On any given Sunday, any team can win." Today, it's more like, "In any given season, anyone can go to the Super Bowl."

Trouble is, parity today means so-so football. Most of the 28 teams play just well enough to beat most of the others. There are no super teams. Super teams that run over other teams aren't all bad. The Green Bay Packers who won Super Bowls I and II were a super team. The Miami Dolphins of the early 1970's were a super team. The Pittsburgh Steelers of the late 1970's (four Super Bowl wins) were a super team. It was fun to watch these guys work. It was a thrill when an underdog beat them. But there are no super teams today.

In preparing for this edition of *Bruce Weber's Inside Pro Football*, we began by studying each division closely. We found a few teams that were clearly better than their "local" rivals. That includes Chicago and Minnesota in the NFC Central, Washington and New York in the NFC East, Cleveland in the AFC Central, San Francisco in the NFC West, and New England in the AFC East.

Since there are no sure things, not even those clubs have a lock on their divisions. But the rest of the NFL teams are loaded with problems.

Look at the AFC West. The Giants and Redskins have proven Denver's problems — defense and running game. The Raiders haven't erased their question mark at quarterback. San Diego has developed one at the same position — Dan Fouts retired, and the Chargers traded for Mark Malone. The folks in Pittsburgh don't believe it. Seattle's offense is far from set. And Kansas City is still trying to figure out the reasons behind its 1986 play-off appearance. You pick 'em.

In the AFC Central, Cincinnati seems to have talent, maybe enough to catch Cleveland. But can coach Sam Wyche direct that talent? Pittsburgh lost Malone (a plus), but are Bubby Brister or Todd Blackledge any better? Houston, an '87 play-off entry, has major problems on defense.

The AFC East is the best example of parity. Two weeks before the end of the '87 season, every team had a decent shot at the play-offs. The Jets have canned a half-dozen one-time stars. The Bills hope that their defense has gained enough experience. The Dolphins hope their defense shows up. And the Colts hope that '87 was not a mirage.

San Francisco has a chance to rebuild while maintaining its edge in the NFC West, but it won't be easy. Age is becoming a factor for coach Bill Walsh. The Saints could be the team to beat in the division. But they're hardly world-beaters. The Rams have a few problems, notably asking whether the 1987 Charles White is the *real* Charles White. The less said about Atlanta, the better.

In the NFC Central, Chicago and Minnesota are years ahead of their opponents. Tampa Bay is coming fastest of all, with Green Bay and Detroit struggling.

Philadelphia has the best chance of joining the Redskins and Giants at the top of the NFC East. The Cardinals will spend some time adjusting to their new Arizona home. The Cowboys will spend more time adjusting to their role as "just another team."

With all of this in mind, we start on the road to Miami the day before Labor Day. The Giants-Redskins Monday-night opener might indicate the strength of the NFC, at least in the east. It's a long road, especially if the folks in Florida don't finish the roads that lead to Joe Robbie Stadium, home of Super Bowl XXIII.

As usual, we won't duck the pressure. Assuming that Bill Parcells works out his offensive line woes, make it the Giants in the NFC. They'll be the first team anywhere to go from first to last to first in three seasons. In the AFC, we'll stick with Cleveland, who should have gone to Super Bowls XXI and XXII. They would have done a better job than Denver in either game.

— Bruce Weber

National Football League All-Pro Team

Wide Receiver
JERRY RICE
SAN FRANCISCO 49ERS

There are good players and there are great players. Then there are "the standards." Jerry Rice of the 49ers is a standard. His abilities set the standard by which all other wide receivers are judged.

The three-year veteran is simply unreal. He does things on a football field — faking, sliding, running, gliding — that no one else can. He had a great reputation when he arrived from tiny Mississippi Valley College in 1985. But no one knew what he could do against top-notch competition. Now they do.

Despite the strike, which limited Rice and the regular Niners to only 12 games, Jerry set an all-time NFL record for TD catches with 22. That's nearly two for every game he played. He also accounted for 1,078 yards, a 16.6 yards-per-catch average.

Flash is the name of Rice's game. He's not the fastest wide receiver in the NFL, but he's certainly not slow. He may be the quickest WR, and that's a major advantage. Jerry is also a flashy dresser off the field and one of the flashiest end-zone dancers following every TD catch. He has developed a sense of flash with the press, too. The standard — in every phase of the game: That's Jerry Rice!

2

Wide Receiver
ANTHONY CARTER
MINNESOTA VIKINGS

One of these days, Anthony Carter is going to play for a team that really knows how to use him. Forgetting his USFL days, Carter has always been a secondary tool.

At the U. of Michigan, coach Bo Schembechler has always preferred to run the football. And at Minnesota, the Vikings sometimes treat A.C. as just another receiver. Don't believe it. This guy is incredible.

In truth, Bo knew it at Michigan. Carter set an all-time school record with 161 catches. And the Vikings also know how dangerous he is. Still, Jerry Burns, Minny's coach, should be thinking about new ways to get the ball to A.C. Last year, Carter caught 38 balls, 53 fewer than NFL champion J.T. Smith (91). But he gained 922 yards on those catches, for an unreal 24.3 yards per catch. No one in the league came close!

"I'm disappointed we didn't get Anthony the ball more often last year," says Burns. "Trouble is, he gets so much coverage that we can't try to force the ball into him. I know if we can get the ball to him more often, it will help our passing game overall."

Al Toon fans may object. Their guy caught 68 passes for the mediocre Jets. But we'll stick with Minny's holy terror, A.C.

Tight End
MARK BAVARO
NEW YORK GIANTS

Things should get a lot better at Giants Stadium this year. That means tight end Mark Bavaro can take another Giant step toward becoming a pro football legend.

Bavaro does the two things tight ends have to do, and he does them better than anyone in the game. He's an awesome blocker. The tougher his assigned opponent is, the more Mark likes to block him. He really enjoys cleaning up on linebackers, and that will help make the Giant running game go.

The one-time Danvers (MA) High School and U. of Notre Dame star is also QB Phil Simms's favorite receiver. When the Giants need key through-the-air yardage, you can look for Bavaro over the middle. One of the strongest tight ends ever, Bavaro usually hangs onto the ball if he can get even one hand on it.

The press calls the 25-year-old "quiet." In truth, he's just a little shy. But with his friends (and even some sportswriters), Mark is a lot more open.

Despite the Giants' awful '87 (6–6 in non-strike games), Bavaro caught 55 passes for 867 yards and 8 TDs. His 15.8 yards per catch were outstanding for a TE. His '88 numbers could be even better.

Tackle
GARY ZIMMERMAN
MINNESOTA VIKINGS

Fans of the New York Giants still don't understand it. After an outstanding career at the U. of Oregon and success with the USFL's Memphis Showboats, Gary Zimmerman was the top Giant choice in the draft of USFL players. In fact, he was the third player chosen. Unfortunately for the Giants (especially with their current problems on the offensive line), Gary didn't want to play in New York (or New Jersey!).

Left with little choice, the Giants dealt Zimmerman to the Vikings on draft day, 1986. Gary stepped right in and helped shore up the Viking offensive line. He must receive much credit for the Vikes' run toward the Super Bowl that fell one game short.

The huge 6–6, 280-pounder combines everything a top pro tackle needs: strength, quickness, sound fundamental skills, and the smarts it takes to execute those skills. *Sports Illustrated* pro football expert Paul Zimmerman has been a Gary Zimmerman fan ever since Gary got to the NFL — though they are not related. Now everyone is jumping on the bandwagon. Gary, whose hobby is aircraft piloting, must scare coach Jerry Burns to death. He scares opponents enough to be an All-Pro and Pro Bowl regular.

Tackle
ANTHONY MUNOZ
CINCINNATI BENGALS

When you pick an All-Pro football team, you almost automatically start with Anthony Munoz. Of course, if Anthony Munoz were picking the team, he probably wouldn't. The 6-6, 278-pounder from Southern Cal isn't satisfied with his performance. He never is. "Once you get the recognition I've gotten, people expect you never to give up a sack," he says. "They expect that you'll never allow your man to make the tackle. That's the standard I set for myself. But I know that the defense is working just as hard as I am."

Anthony underrates himself. He's just about at that standard. He allowed only 1½ sacks last year, a nearly perfect grade. He did it with a rotator cuff injury suffered on November 8 that required surgery in January. But it didn't keep him off the field.

His line coach, Jim McNally, notes that Anthony no longer dominates every play of every game. "The defensive people are now as big as he is. But he's still the best athlete I've ever been around. He has outstanding agility and quickness. He's probably the most athletic lineman in the league." When you remember that the guy weighs around 280 pounds, you know why he is still the best.

6

Guard
MIKE MUNCHAK
HOUSTON OILERS

For years, the Oilers have toiled in secret. Locked in at the bottom of the so-so AFC Central Division, fans outside the shadow of the Astrodome rarely saw an Oiler game on TV. Neither did the media. Neither did the other NFL players. *Monday Night Football*? Not a chance.

That also means that few football-types ever got to see Mike Munchak play. Too bad. The 6–3, 280-pound Munchak plays guard the way it was meant to be played. Trouble is, if the press and players can't see him play, he is often overlooked for special honors.

Those days are ending. The Oilers figure to be right in the thick of the AFC Central fight, following their 1987 play-off run. That could mean TV exposure — and a sense of how good Mike Munchak really is.

After only six seasons, Mike is the senior Oiler. He was their top draft pick in 1982, following a stint under Joe Paterno at Penn State.

Actually, Mike has played in three Pro Bowls, starting the last two for the AFC. Not bad for a guy who has played before some of the game's smallest crowds. *Pro Football Weekly* named Mike the NFL's top guard last year. We agree.

Guard
TOM NEWBERRY
LOS ANGELES RAMS

When Tom Newberry arrived in the Ram camp, he certainly didn't have much going for him. He came out of a small college program at Wisconsin-LaCrosse. He hadn't played against the type of lineman he would face in the NFL. He was 6-2 in a land of 6-5 and 6-6 guys. And he was coming into a pro program that enjoyed a tradition of super linemen.

That didn't stop Newberry. First, Tom was tremendously strong, coming out of college, and has continued to get even stronger. He's nearly tops among the pros in that department. Then there's his "wing span." With a 74-inch spread from fingertip to fingertip with his arms outstretched, Newberry has the reach of a 6-7 man. Finally, there are his work habits. No one outworks the young Ram.

Ram coach John Robinson is among Newberry's biggest fans. "He reminds me a lot of [ex-Ram guard] Dennis Harrah," says the head Ram. High praise indeed. "Tom is a thinking man's lineman and he's very physical. That's an unusual combination. Too many people think if you can do one, you can't do the other." For Newberry, it means that he knows what he has to do on every play — and does it!

Center
RAY DONALDSON
INDIANAPOLIS COLTS

Indianapolis coach Ron Meyer never takes the easy way out. Ask him about his center, Ray Donaldson, and he tells you straight out: "Ray Donaldson is, without a doubt, the best center in the NFL. He is our most valuable player. He has been for quite a while. I'd hate to think where we would be without Ray and his leadership abilities."

High praise indeed. And why not? The 6–3, 288-pounder has put together two straight Pro Bowl seasons. It isn't easy, playing in the same division as everyone's All-Pro, Dwight Stephenson of the Dolphins. Now, with Stephenson's ability to come back from a tough knee injury in question, Donaldson zooms right to the top of most All-Pro lists.

The one-time U. of Georgia star was the 32nd player selected in the 1980 NFL draft. Except for the three-game strike last season, he has played in every Colt game. In fact, he hasn't missed a play in the last two years, the only Colt to do so. His play makes the whole line better.

Unlike many clubs, the Colts have rushed for 2,000 or more yards in four of the last five seasons. Ray Donaldson makes that happen.

Quarterback
DAN
MARINO
MIAMI DOLPHINS

We'll get some arguments about this one, for sure. Dan Marino has had better years than he had in '87. Joe Montana was never better, in his first full season after back surgery. John Elway, with little running help, got Denver a second straight Super Bowl trip. But this is our 1988 All-Pro team, and we'll stick with the guy who has done it all for so long now.

That's our man, Dan Marino. When the chips are down, we'd like to have the ball in his hands. He doesn't get much more help than Elway. (Troy Stradford may change all that.) He doesn't have a receiver like Montana's Jerry Rice. (The Dolphins' Marks brothers aren't shabby.) But look at what Marino has done.

The ex-U. of Pitt star has started 69 of his 71 career games. He has hit on 1,512 of 2,494 passes (60.6%) for 19,422 yards and thrown for 168 TDs. His career rating of 94.1 is the best ever in the NFL. He has thrown for four or more TDs 14 times, trailing only Johnny Unitas (17). Only recently retired Dan Fouts of San Diego has more 300-yard games.

If his center, Dwight Stephenson, doesn't return from knee surgery, Marino's life could get tougher. But Dan Marino thrives on tough.

Running Back
ERIC DICKERSON
INDIANAPOLIS COLTS

No one in Anaheim, CA, gets to vote for our All-Pro team. Good thing for Eric Dickerson. The one-time Pony from SMU (now a Colt from Indianapolis) didn't leave many friends in the L.A. area when he forced the Rams to deal him somewhere, anywhere.

But Eric will more than make up for it in Indy. His arrival marked a gigantic turn-around for the Colts, who had scraped along the bottom of the AFC East for years. With Eric toting the ball, the Colts did something they had never before done in Indiana — win the division title.

Problem is, Eric does super things on the field (he always has). But he gets involved in all sorts of troubles off it. He has had problems with coaches beginning in high school, and he has gone through at least three agents in his pro career.

Still, reunited with one-time SMU coach Ron Meyer at Indy, Dickerson seems happy. "I had to get out of L.A.," says Eric, who still lives there in the off-season. And his '87 numbers, basically in Indianapolis (1,288 yards and six TDs) indicate that his move was right — at least for him.

With his goggles flashing in the lights, Dickerson is scary-looking on the field. With the ball in his hands, he's even scarier.

11

Running Back
CHARLES WHITE
LOS ANGELES RAMS

When Charles White left Southern Cal, Heisman Trophy in hand, his future looked brilliant. A future All-Pro? Why not? Among the USC tailbacks who went on to great pro feats, White was as good as any.

A year ago, it was another story. White had wandered through the NFL and was just barely hanging on with the Rams. His old college coach, John Robinson, was the Ram boss. He had one final chance. He almost blew it in August 1987. He was nabbed, high on drugs. Now, he must be tested every week. One failure can cost him his career. Charles White is not about to blow it again.

One year later, Charles White is an All-Pro and, given the Rams' ability to block for the run, likely to be one again in '88.

"Given my problems," says White, "I'm lucky to be alive." The Rams are, too. When Eric Dickerson forced his trade to Indianapolis, Robinson turned full-time to White, who really responded.

Charles, who played in the strike games, led the NFL in rushing with 1,374 yards and a 4.2-yards-per-carry average. Only the Jets' Johnny Hector scored as many rushing TDs (11). Yes, Charles White has it all together now.

Defensive End
BRUCE SMITH
BUFFALO BILLS

Buffalo fans have suffered long enough. There have been too many awful years. But the wait may be over, thanks to a formerly overly large defensive bookend named Bruce Smith. Yes, the Buffalo defense is in great hands with Smith and youngsters Shane Conlan and Cornelius Bennett.

The latter two just arrived last year. Smith has been around awhile. But he made a bigger impression on Buffalo's fast-food restaurants than he did in its stadium. And he played like an overstuffed bag of McDonald's burgers.

Buffalo fans expected more. They had been disappointed by top draft choices before. But this big fellow from Virginia Tech arrived with all sorts of great press notices.

It took the arrival of new coach Marv Levy to turn things around for Smith. Bruce slimmed down to a neat 285 pounds and began pounding opposing QBs into the turf (natural and artificial). Now, instead of sleeping late and tanking up at the table, Smith spends his off-hours running and lifting.

"Smith is the best defensive end in the league," raves Denver's John Elway, who knows from firsthand experience.

Defensive Tackle
STEVE McMICHAEL
CHICAGO BEARS

The best free-agent pickup the Chicago Bears have ever made? Here's a vote for defensive tackle Steve McMichael. A Patriot No. 3 choice in 1980, McMichael was dropped by New England and picked up by Chicago in 1981. The rest, as they say, is history.

By 1983 he was in the Bear starting lineup. He became one of Chicago's sack leaders (second with 8½ that first full season). The honors came quickly in the following years: All-NFC; All-NFL; and after the 1986 season, the Pro Bowl. Now with a couple of Pro Bowl seasons behind him, he anchors that rugged Bear defense.

There's nothing glamorous about playing in the middle of the defensive line. It's tough work, but Steve makes the most of it. In the Bears' last game last year, a loss to Washington in the play-offs, his fumble recovery set up the first Bear TD. Steve also had a career-high 12 tackles and three sacks in last December's Minnesota game. He was named NFC defensive player of the week.

Not exactly routine for the 6–2, 265-pounder, but no shock either. If you know that Steve lists rattlesnake hunting as a favorite hobby, you know he's tough.

14

Defensive End
REGGIE WHITE
PHILADELPHIA EAGLES

Hang around the Eagle locker room and you may hear the voices of Rodney Dangerfield, Muhammad Ali, or Clint Eastwood. You may hear a German shepherd barking loudly. But you'll find neither celebrity nor dog in the area. It's just super defensive end (and sometimes tackle) Reggie White entertaining his teammates.

The one-time U. of Tennessee and USFL Memphis Showboats star does little entertaining on the field. He's a destruction machine, who forces every opposing coach to redesign his pass-blocking schemes. "If you've got a running back out there on Reggie," says Washington coach Joe Gibbs, "forget it. Your QB is going down."

The 6–5, 285-pounder owned the NFL sack department last season. His 21 sacks were 8½ better than the runners-up, the Bears' Richard Dent and the Pats' Andre Tippett. In fact he missed the NFL sack record (22 by Mark Gastineau) by only one, despite playing four games fewer than the Jet star.

White is extremely religious. At Tennessee, he was called "The Minister of Defense." Philly boss Buddy Ryan, White's biggest fan, moves him around on the line. That way he scares everyone on the other team.

Outside Linebacker
CARL BANKS
NEW YORK GIANTS

Attention please, dear readers. Attention please. It's the least we can do for Carl Banks. The Giants' great linebacker isn't exactly unknown. But when you play opposite Lawrence Taylor, you just don't get much attention.

Let's hope this does it for Carl. The one-time Michigan State star has put together three outstanding seasons for the Super Bowl XXI champs. "I don't really care about recognition," says the 6–4, 235-pounder. "I just go out and play as hard as I can whenever I'm in there."

Though both Banks and Taylor play OLB for the same team, they have totally different assignments. L.T. is the pressure man on the opposing quarterback. Banks forces the run, covers on passes, and stuffs the tight end. Carl's job isn't nearly as glamorous as Taylor's. But, as he says, "I just want to do my job as well as I can."

Last year was Banks's first Pro Bowl season. Many, including Carl, thought he deserved it during the Giants' championship season. "I guess you have to have more than one good season to make it," he says.

Maybe so. But any player who works as hard as Carl does week in and week out has many Pro Bowl seasons in his future.

Inside Linebacker
FREDD YOUNG
SEATTLE SEAHAWKS

If you spell Fredd Young properly, you mustn't forget the two d's in Fredd. To evaluate his playing performance, you should probably spell it "greattt."

In four seasons with the Seahawks, Fredd has been to the Pro Bowl four times. The first two times he was selected for his ability on special teams. The last two, it was a salute to his work at inside linebacker. In fact, he is the first Seattle linebacker ever selected for the Pro Bowl

He's a one-man wrecking crew for the men of Chuck Knox. As usual, he led the team in tackles (101 in 13 games), including 10 or more against the Lions (14), Raiders (13), Broncos (12), and Jets (10). There's nothing new there. Fredd was the leading tackler and MVP at New Mexico State, too.

Seattle makes its living on the number of takeaways. Fredd shines there. In 1987, he forced five fumbles and recovered another four. He also had an interception and nine quarterback sacks. Not bad. He does it under pressure, too. In the AFC Wild Card game, he had 12 tackles, forced a fumble, and recovered another.

The native of Dallas is all over the place for the Seahawks. And he is plenty tough. (Make that "toughhh.")

17

Inside Linebacker
MIKE
SINGLETARY
CHICAGO BEARS

Mike Singletary has always been one of the quicker linebackers in the NFL. Now, maybe he's too quick. Late last season, Mike signed a new contract with the Bears that put him into the highest-paid class of NFL linebackers — at that time.

Singletary is a terror on the field and a pussycat off it. But his off-the-field manner had to change when his teammate, Wilber Marshall, signed a free-agent pact with the Washington Redskins. Instantly, Marshall went to the highest-paid class, passing Mike — and Lawrence Taylor and Hugh Green.

No matter. Mike will be back behind the Chicago defensive line this fall, doing his thing better than anyone else in the game.

Singletary's off-field heroics benefit lots of folks in Chicago who need his help. On the field, it's usually the opponents who are hollering for help. As pro linebackers go, Singletary is a dwarf. At 5–11½ and only 228 pounds, Mike doesn't have all the physical tools. But if there's a smarter inside LB in the game, we haven't found him yet.

"Leadership is what makes Mike great," says another Mike, Bear coach Mike Ditka. "He makes everyone around him play better."

Outside Linebacker
ANDRE TIPPETT
NEW ENGLAND PATRIOTS

These have not been the best of times in New England. For a long while, the Patriots were deep in money trouble. But there's joy on every fan's face now. No. 56 will be back, doing his thing. That's Andre Tippett and, frankly, the guy's a monster.

The 1987 season marked hard-hitting Andre's fourth straight Pro Bowl season. The 6–3, 241-pounder was the Pats' fourth-leading tackler (83, including 53 first-hits), and he led the club in fumble recoveries with three. The highlight: a 29-yard TD return against the Jets. Rival quarterbacks certainly don't relish seeing Tippett across the line. Only Lawrence Taylor, Dexter Manley, Mark Gastineau, and Jacob Green own more all-time sacks than Tippett, the one-time Newark (NJ) high school star.

Off the field, Tippett leads a varied life. He's a second-degree black belt in karate, AFC East rivals should know. And he also spends leisure time in target shooting, bowling, and cooking. Variety has always been the name of Andre's game. He wrestled and took part in track and field in high school (in addition to football, of course). And he played both defensive end and linebacker for his college team, the U. of Iowa.

Cornerback
HANFORD DIXON
CLEVELAND BROWNS

See the smile on Marty Schottenheimer's face. Smile, Marty, smile. Why is this man smiling? Simply because as head coach of the Cleveland Browns, he knows that defense starts with good cornerbacks. Smiling Marty has two of the best. In fact he has both All-Pro cornerbacks, Hanford Dixon and Frank Minnifield.

The Pro Bowl starter (along with his teammate), Dixon is a seven-year veteran who played in his 101st career game in last season's all-important finale with Pittsburgh. How did the one-time Southern Mississippi star do? He had a season-high five solo tackles. He caused one fumble. He picked off his third pass of the season (and the 23rd of his career). Just another day at the office.

Dixon spends lots of time in the Browns' offices, usually in the film room. When Schottenheimer was the Browns' defensive boss, he used to kid Dixon. "He knew I had lots of talent," remembers the 5–11, 186-pounder. "He used to worry about my preparation."

Now Dixon is one of the most prepared players in the league. He pours over film and videotape of his upcoming opponent. Now almost no one gets past him.

Cornerback
FRANK MINNIFIELD
CLEVELAND BROWNS

When Frank Minnifield got to his first Pro Bowl game in 1986, he wasn't happy. He had been "appointed" to the team by AFC (and Brown) coach Marty Schottenheimer. "I wasn't comfortable," remembers the 5–9, 180-pounder from Louisville. "It was like I didn't belong."

Frank was back in the Pro Bowl in 1987, elected by the AFC coaches. Now he belonged. We believe he'll belong again in '88 — and for years to come. He certainly has the numbers. He intercepted three Warren Moon passes (tying a club record) one afternoon last November. He had a season-high 10 tackles the following week against San Francisco. He defensed three passes and helped limit the Raiders' wide men to only five catches.

Minnifield has a fan in Brown all-timer Jim Brown. "I like little guys who attack, who hit instead of being hit," says Brown, who dished out punishment well during his career. "Guys like Minnifield and Dixon, they have the attitude."

Frank likes playing aggressively. "I don't want to talk about the other team's wide receivers. I don't even want to know their names. I just want them to know Frank Minnifield after we're finished playing."

Strong Safety
JOEY BROWNER
MINNESOTA VIKINGS

The most aggressive strong safety in pro football? It's Joey Browner of the Vikings. The best strong safety in the NFL? Same guy, though we expect some arguments.

The three-time Pro Bowler is one of the hardest hitters in the game. Sometimes he gets carried away. Though he has never really hurt the Viking team efforts, his critics feel that he could someday.

"Nonsense," says Browner. "I'm out there playing the game as hard as I can. If someone gets the wrong idea, that's too bad."

Martial arts training has given Joey a pair of the toughest hands in football. One hand tackle, which saved a touchdown against Denver, broke Gerald Willhite's leg.

Hard hitting also scares opponents. "Players just don't like going into his area," says Bear coach Mike Ditka.

Browner is one of the best special teams coverage men in the league. That's what got him his first Pro Bowl shot. But Browner isn't happy playing on the specials while he's a full-time free safety. "He'll be out there when I need him," says Vike coach Jerry Burns.

If rookie Brad Edwards can step in at free safety for Minnesota, he and Browner will make things even better for the Vikes.

Free Safety
RONNIE LOTT
SAN FRANCISCO 49ERS

Think about the 49ers and you think offense. Coach Bill Walsh is an offensive genius. WR Jerry Rice floats down the field to make a great catch. RB Roger Craig, running and catching, gains 1,307 yards. But in the NFL, you win with defense. In San Francisco, that starts with Ronnie Lott.

A hard hitter? That's Ronnie Lott. A smart, heady player? That's also Ronnie Lott. He's tough enough to play hurt — and to hurt the opponents, too. He's also a good enough athlete to move from cornerback (where he was a Pro Bowler for four seasons) to free safety (where he has been a Pro Bowler for two seasons).

The move to safety placed defensive leadership responsibilities squarely on his relatively small shoulder pads. At only 6–0 and 200 pounds, Lott still dishes out some of the hardest hits in the league. In '87, he was the Niners' third-leading tackler (55), behind a pair of linebackers. He also picked off five passes (returned for 62 yards) and defensed another 10 tosses.

Even more revealing, Lott forced three of the 16 fumbles the entire club created all season. He recovered one for a 33-yard return. Coach Walsh wishes he had lots of Lotts.

Can ex-Ram Eric Dickerson lead the Colts
to a second-straight AFC East title?

American Football Conference Team Previews

AFC East
NEW ENGLAND PATRIOTS
1987 Finish: Second
1988 Prediction: First

Ronnie Lippett　　　　　　　　　　　**Garin Veris**

Peace, it seems, is finally at hand in New England. Reebok's Paul Fireman has stepped in to bail out the cash-short Sullivan family, which solves a bunch of Patriot problems. LB Andre Tippett will stay on with the Pats, and the players will be paid on time. Even coach Ray Berry will hang on for another go-round.

That's good news. The Pats may well be the AFC East's most talented bunch, once they sort out the problems. Start with QB. Steve Grogan was the Pat hero last year, shaking off serious injuries to win in the clutch late in the year. But Tony Eason may well return to the helm. Ex-USFLers Tom Ramsey and Doug Flutie, both of whom saw action for New England last year, also join the battle. At least one will go.

If Craig James bounces back from the injured list, the running game will be in better shape. Vet Tony Collins returns from a season in which he led the Pats in rushing (474 yards) and receptions (44 for 347 yards). Mosi Tatupu returns for his 11th season, along with Bob Perryman, Reggie Dupard, and top pick John Stephens.

WR Stanley Morgan must bounce back from a season-ending injury to join talented-but-much-troubled Irving Fryar, Cedric Jones, and Stephen Starring. TE Lin Dawson is first-rate, with help from Willie Scott.

Up front, second-year Ts Bruce Armstrong and Danny Villa provide future security. LG Sean Farrell is outstanding.

DRE Garin Veris and LOLB Tippett are the forces that make the defense go. DLE Ken Sims and NT Toby Williams join Veris up front, with Brent Williams, Milford Hodge, and Mike Ruth ready to help.

Linebacker is a key spot for New England with LILB Steve Nelson retired and ROLB Don Blackmon gone (injury). Ed Williams, Ed Reynolds, and Johnny Rembert must be ready.

The secondary is experienced. SS Roland James bounced back from a knee injury to star opposite FS Fred Marion. RCB Ray Clayborn must rebound from a freak injury to rejoin LCB Ronnie Lippett.

Pat special teams were so-so last year, with punter Rich Camarillo possibly the top man on the unit.

AFC East
INDIANAPOLIS COLTS
1987 Finish: First
1988 Prediction: Second

Bill Brooks   **Duane Bickett**

The 1987 AFC East title was a tribute to
the arrival of super RB Eric Dickerson,
improved offensive line play, and just a
pinch or two of old-fashioned luck. Coach
Ron Meyer knows that a repeat title — and
another step toward the Super Bowl — will
require further changes.

Dickerson (1,011 yards for the Colts and
1,288 overall) made the Indy running game.
But the price was high; and without draft
picks, Meyer's building job will be more
difficult.

The QB picture is cloudy. Oft-injured
Gary Hogeboom is probably the better
player. Jack Trudeau has good days and
not-so-good days. The Colts may trade for
a new arm. The receivers, led by Bill Brooks
(51 for 722 yards) and Matt Bouza (42 for 569

yards), are fairly good. The No. 3 receiver, Albert Bentley (34 for 477), is also an outstanding running back (142 for 631).

The secret to the Colts' offensive improvement is the line. C Ray Donaldson is the leader. If Miami's Dwight Stephenson doesn't make it back from last year's season-ending injury, Donaldson becomes the league's class center. RG Ron Solt enjoyed his first Pro Bowl year, and LT Chris Hinton is among the league's best. Ben Utt is solid at LG, with Kevin Call set at RT.

Aggressiveness is the watchword of the improved Colt defense. Former top draftee Duane Bickett keyed the stop unit with his work against the run and his pass-rush in nickel defense situations.

The play of Barry Krauss (off surgery and illness) at right inside 'backer fired up the whole unit. Donnell Thompson and Jon Hand are just fine at the ends, with Jerome Sally and a healthy Scott Kellar at the nose.

With Bickett and Krauss dominating on the right side, some forget Johnie Cooks and Cliff Odom on the left. It's a fine linebacker crew.

The secondary is fairly set with LCB Willie Tullis and RCB Eugene Daniel joining SS Nesby Glasgow and FS Freddie Robinson.

There are questions about the punting game where P Rohn Stark just hasn't bloomed. PK Dean Biasucci is the AFC's Pro Bowler. Albert Bentley is fine as a kickoff returner.

AFC East
BUFFALO BILLS
1987 Finish: Fourth
1988 Prediction: Third

Cornelius Bennett   **Shane Conlan**

"Dee-fense! Dee-fense! Dee-fense!" That's the favorite call in Rich Stadium, Buffalo, these days. The Bills have the makings of an awesome defense. Fact is, the club may be just a player or three away from rocking the AFC East.

Under coach Marv Levy, the Bills have taken a giant step toward the "promised land." The offense is in capable hands with QB Jim Kelly. And the arrival of Shane Conlan and Cornelius Bennett as rookie LBs made DE Bruce Smith a Pro Bowler. There will be exciting times in Buffalo. Maybe not this year, but soon.

Despite late-season losses to New England and Philadelphia that ended '87 playoff dreams, Kelly showed consistency and leadership, which should make him a premier NFL QB. His '87 numbers (250 for 419, 2,798 yards, 19 TDs, 83.8 rating) were good and could get better.

Young runners like Ronnie Harmon (116 for 485) and Jamie Mueller (82 for 354) show promise, though the ground game must improve. Top draft pick Thurman Thomas may help.

The receivers, led by Chris Burkett and Andre Reed, come off a fine year; and Pete Metzelaars is okay at TE, though he must cut down on his fumbles and holding calls.

The offensive line is small by NFL standards, which hurt the Bills late in the season. Depth is needed behind tackles Will Wolford and Joe Devlin, guards Jim Ritcher and Tim Vogler, and center Kent Hull.

DRE Bruce Smith is second only to Philly's Reggie White among NFL DEs. NT Fred Smerlas is the veteran of the young defensive group, which includes DLE Sean McNanie and backups Leon Seals, Dean Prater, and Bruce Mesner.

The entire defense benefits from the play of '87 rookies ILB Shane Conlan and LOLB Cornelius Bennett. They made better players out of ROLB Darryl Talley and ILB Scott Radecic.

The play up front took some pressure off a so-so secondary. FS Mark Kelso was one of Buffalo's most improved players. SS Ron Pitts and corners Derrick Burroughs and Nate Odomes should return.

Pro Bowl special teamer Steve Tasker keys one of the league's best units.

AFC East
MIAMI DOLPHINS
1987 Finish: Third
1988 Prediction: Fourth

John Offerdahl   **Troy Stradford**

It's the same old story at Miami. Not
enough defense. Coach Don Shula remains
the game's sharpest. QB Dan Marino can
still put plenty of points on the board. And
the running game, with star rookie Troy
Stradford, shows signs of giving the offense
balance. But the defense can't get the job
done, which will keep the home team out
of Super Bowl XXIII at Robbie Stadium.

Marino is still the NFL's most dangerous
thrower. He hit on 263 of 444 a year ago for
3,245 yards and 26 TDs. Just another year
for the ex-Pitt dandy. There were four other
QBs on the Miami roster in '87, just in case.
No case.

WRs Mark Clayton and Mark Duper, the
famous Miami Marks brothers, were limited to 79 catches between them last sea-

son, accounting for 15 TDs. They've had better seasons. TE Bruce Hardy added another 28.

The top receiver? Surprise RB Troy Stradford. The one-time Boston College standout caught 48 tosses for 457 yards. He also ripped off 619 ground yards (145 carries) to lead the "Fish" in that area. Continued progress could key a Dolphin comeback.

The return of C Dwight Stephenson, long the NFL's best, is a key to the offensive line. It's questionable. If he can't go, look for Jeff Dellenbach, joined by tackles Jon Geisler and Ronnie Lee, and guards Roy Foster and Tom Toth.

In Tom Olivadotti's second year as defensive coordinator, look for changes at outside linebacker. Injuries have ruined Hugh Green, while age has done in Bob Brudzinski. Youngsters Rick Graf and Mark Brown may get the call. RILB John Offerdahl is a Pro Bowler, and LILB Jackie Shipp could be pressured by Scott Nicolas. Top pick Eric Kumerow may be a year away.

Vet Doug Betters isn't (better, that is), so young John Bosa figures as the next great Dolphin DE. DE T.J. Turner and NT Brian Sochia will have to improve.

SS Glenn Blackwood's best days are behind him. The position is wide open. Corners Paul Lankford and Williams Judson and free safety Bud Brown must get better for Miami to move up from No. 26 in the league on defense.

AFC East
NEW YORK JETS
1987 Finish: Fifth
1988 Prediction: Fifth

Ken O'Brien   **Al Toon**

As the sad '87 season wound down, Jet fans hollered for coach Joe Walton's scalp. "Joe must go, Joe must go!" they screamed. Owner Leon Hess wasn't listening. Joe stayed. Lots of the fans' old favorites went, however, including DT Joe Klecko, C Joe Fields, P Dave Jennings, T Gordon King, and DE Barry Bennett. They'll sell lots of programs to Jet fans this fall.

Both player and coaching staff changes will give the Jets a new look. Whether it's a better look remains to be seen. The Jets started well the past two seasons, then sank sharply.

Injuries took a heavy toll in '87. QB Ken O'Brien is reliable, and backup Pat Ryan is solid. Freeman McNeil (121 for 530) no longer dominates a game, but Johnny Hector (111 for 435) is always a threat. Rookie Roger Vick (77 for 257) will help.

There's nothing wrong with WR Al Toon (68 for 976), one of the game's best, but Wesley Walker (9 for 190) is sliding downhill. TE Mickey Shuler (43 for 434) can do it.

With Fields gone and RG Dan Alexander in trouble, the offensive line will be well shaken in '88. The Jets have drafted poorly in recent years, which will continue to hurt. Ts Jim Sweeney and Reggie McElroy should return, along with Guy Bingham and Ted Banker. Huge top pick Dave Cadigan should move right in.

Walton's defense has been awful. He brought in more coaching help, but the line may be starting from scratch with Klecko and Bennett gone, and ends Marty Lyons and Mark Gastineau coming off horrid years. End Scott Mersereau and tackle Gerald Nichols enjoyed good rookie seasons and may be the men of the future. Tom Baldwin is a key.

The linebacking is just as sad. Lance Mehl finished '87 on the injured list, leaving Bob Crable to lead a so-so group. Alex Gordon was '87's top rookie at his LOLB spot, but guys like Troy Benson, Kevin McArthur, and Kyle Clifton must improve.

The Jets hope that CBs Russell Carter and Kerry Glenn return healthy. FS Harry Hamilton, and SS Lester Lyles and Rich Miano need help from a pass-rush that never happened last year. Draftees Terry Williams and Sheldon White should help.

AFC Central
CLEVELAND BROWNS
1987 Finish: First
1988 Prediction: First

Webster Slaughter   **Bernie Kosar**

We believe that the Browns should have gone to the last two Super Bowls. Narrow losses to Denver prevented both journeys. But does anyone believe that Cleveland would have done any worse than the Broncos in losses to the Giants and the Redskins?

What do the Browns have to do to finally get a Super Bowl ring? Not much. Coach Marty Schottenheimer must find a week-in, week-out punter. And he should try to improve his defensive line, with Carl Hairston ready for his 14th season.

With offensive coordinator Lindy Infante off to coach the Packers, QB Bernie Kosar's college QB coach, Mark Trestman, gets the call. Kosar (62% completions, 7.8 yards per attempt, AFC-leading 95.4 rating) isn't a classic QB. He rarely makes mistakes.

Cleveland runs the ball about as often as they pass it. And why not? Pro Bowler Kevin Mack (735 yards) and Earnest Byner (432 yards) are an outstanding pair, though Cleveland fans can't forget Byner's last-second championship-game fumble. It's time to forget.

Kosar's top receiver is Byner (52 for 552). But his wideouts are young and talented. Everyone loves Reggie Langhorne, Webster Slaughter, and Brian Brennan. TE Ozzie Newsome, ready for his 11th year, caught 34 balls last year. Derek Tennell backs up.

The offensive front is an experienced group, including Ts Paul Farren and Cody Risien, Gs Larry Williams and Dan Fike, and C Mike Babb. It's a good group.

As a unit, the defense is one of the NFL's best. It's not a great sacking defense; but the secondary is blessed with great talent, and the front group allowed only one 100-yard rushing performance in '87.

A healthy NT Bob Golic should rejoin end mate Sam Clancy in '88, with excellent support from Reggie Camp and Darryl Sims. If Mike Junkin comes back from serious wrist surgery, he'll rejoin senior Brown Clay Matthews, Lucious Sanford, Eddie Johnson, and Mike Johnson behind the line. Top pick Clifford Charlton should help.

CBs Frank Minnifield and Hanford Dixon are the league's best corner combo. There's nothing wrong with safeties Ray Ellis and Felix Wright.

AFC Central
PITTSBURGH STEELERS
1987 Finish: Third
1988 Prediction: Second

Keith Willis   **Tunch Ilkin**

It's not true that king Chuck Noll has been heard to moan, "A quarterback, a quarterback, my kingdom for a quarterback." Not a bad trade idea, though. Having cleaned up a bunch of defensive problems with great young players, Noll now faces life looking for someone who can run his offense like Terry Bradshaw did.

Mark Malone could never do it. He tossed only six TDs last year with 19 interceptions. The passing game was the league's worst. Is Bubby Brister the man? Is ex-Chief Todd Blackledge? Will Pittsburgh trade for a more experienced QB? It's vital.

'Tis tough to run the ball without a passing game. Still, Earnest Jackson led in rushing again (696 yards, seventh in the AFC). Walter Abercrombie, not the breakaway threat the Steelers need, rushed for 459 yards. Frank Pollard (536 yards) is now the Steelers' No. 4 all-time rusher.

There are possible problems at WR, where future Hall of Famer John Stallworth has retired and Louis Lipps has been banged up. Charles Lockett and Weegie Thompson will feel the pressure. Danzell Lee and vet Preston Gothard will battle at TE.

Frequent All-Pro C Mike Webster unretired after one week to start his 15th season — and that's great news. He'll rejoin guards Craig Wolfley and Terry Long and tackle Tunch Ilkin. Watch for talented John Rienstra to get a shot at left tackle.

The return of Pittsburgh's rock-hard defense marked the '87 season. A major problem in '86, defense was a major asset last year. ROLB Mike Merriweather was the Pittsburgh MVP. He was the third-leading tackler (65), leading sacker (5½), and leading fumble-grabber (3). The other LBs (LOLB Bryan Hinkle, LILB David Little, and RILB Robin Cole) are solid. There's depth, too.

The retirement of SS Donnie Shell could cause a secondary problem, but Thomas Everett made a fine rookie debut at FS. RCB Delton Hall stepped right in at RCB and was the top Steeler rookie. Dwayne Woodruff returns at LCB.

Keith Willis, Gary Dunn, and Edmund Nelson are okay up front. The pass-rush will be improved by top draftee Aaron Jones.

AFC Central
CINCINNATI BENGALS
1987 Finish: Fourth
1988 Prediction: Third

Tim Krumrie   **Boomer Esiason**

One day we expect to turn on our TV to
watch *The Twilight Zone* and see the Cincinnati Bengals' highlight film. This is a
team with a talented offense and a solid
defense. Trouble is, when the offense plays
well, the defense doesn't. When the defense
is on, the offense isn't. And coach Sam
Wyche makes some decisions that are right
out of science fiction.

Shockingly, Wyche will be back for
another year after last season's strange 4–
11 record. Okay, owner Paul Brown knows
more about football coaching than most
living humans, and it's his team. Still,
Wyche had better win early this year.

He should win. Lefty QB Boomer Esiason passed for 3,321 yards in '87, second
only to the Cards' Neil Lomax. WR Eddie

Brown is a reliable receiver (44 for 608 yards), but Boomer (and Cincy) need the return of a healthy Cris Collinsworth. If not, Tim McGee gets the call.

Six Bengals rushed for 200 yards or more in '87, with Larry Kinnebrew (145 for 570 yards) the leader. A healthy James Brooks would help tremendously. Rodney Holman should return at TE.

Despite season-long shoulder woes, LT Anthony Munoz is the best there is. He keys the Bengal offensive line. The rest of the cast, including tackle Joe Walter, guards Bruce Reimers and Max Montoya, and center Dave Rimington, should be back, with backups Brian Blados and Bruce Kozerski.

When you've got a nose tackle who leads your team in tackles, you've got someone special. That's the word for Cincy NT Tim Krumrie, the middle man between Jim Skow and Eddie Edwards. Look for Jason Buck to get another shot at DLE.

Emanuel King and Carl Zander appear set at the left linebacking spots. Reggie Williams, now 34, may give it another shot on the right with Kiki DeAyala.

With Louis Breeden gone, Ray Horton may be back on the right corner. Elsewhere in the secondary, Lewis Billups should return at the left corner with David Fulcher and Robert Jackson at the safeties. The Bengals will find a spot for top draftee, CB Rickey Dixon.

Special teams need work. They cost the Bengals at least two wins a year ago.

AFC Central
HOUSTON OILERS
1987 Finish: Second
1988 Prediction: Fourth

Warren Moon   **Keith Bostic**

Talk to the folks in Houston. You will quickly find that Jerry Glanville is either (1) an outstanding coach who makes the most of limited player talent or (2) a jerk who has outstayed his welcome. Oiler owner Bud Adams believes No. 1, so Glanville is back, looking for a second straight play-off berth.

With few super AFC teams, the man in black has a shot at it. His offense is pretty good (and probably getting better). His defense needs help, but not more than many AFC rivals. If 1987 was a strange season, 1988 could be even stranger.

QB Warren Moon, whose suggestion that Glanville open up the offense during the '86 season has paid off, is developing into a fine NFL passer. Though he hit on only 50% of his tosses last year (184 for 368, 2,806 yards, 21 TDs), he almost always makes the big play. RB Mike Rozier (229 for 957 yards) enjoyed his best year ever. Alonzo Highsmith is back for his first full season, joining top draftee Lorenzo White.

WR Ernest Givins (53 for 933 yards) is outstanding with his opposite number, Drew Hill (49 for 989 yards), not far behind. Jamie Williams is solid at TE.

The Oiler offensive line is loaded with top draft picks, a credit to the front-office crew. Tops is All-Pro LG Mike Munchak. The rest of the crew includes Ts Bruce Davis and Dean Steinkuhler, G Bruce Matthews, and C Jay Pennison.

The Oiler problems come on defense. They can use help at defensive end, where DLE Ray Childress is the line's leading tackler (69) and sacker (6). Doug Smith should return at the nose.

Help is also needed at outside linebacker, where Robert Lyles and Johnny Meads held forth last season. John Grimsley and Al Smith play inside.

The pass defense isn't that good, either. SS Keith Bostic tied for the AFC lead in interceptions (6), earning a trip to the Pro Bowl. Since the Oilers do lots of blitzing, corners Patrick Allen and Steve Brown are forced to play head-up on opposing receivers — and with good results. They do a first-rate job.

Glanville shook up his coaching staff this season, but it will take improved defense for Houston to make the play-offs in '88.

AFC West
SEATTLE SEAHAWKS
1987 Finish: Second
1988 Prediction: First

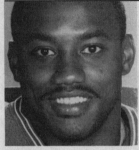 

Curt Warner   **Jacob Green**

Here's one of the toughest clubs to figure. World-beaters one week, wimps the
next, the 'Hawks are driving coach Chuck
Knox crazy. There are problem areas. But
if Seattle puts an entire season together,
they could go to Super Bowl XXIII.

The running game is excellent. Both Curt
Warner (234 for 985 yards) and FB John L.
Williams are solid performers. But there's
no depth. When Warner missed the AFC
play-off tilt with Houston, Seattle was shot.
QB Dave Kreig is a model of inconsistency.
Despite an 87.6 passer rating (178 for 294,
2,131 yards, 23 TDs), Knox never knows
which Kreig will show up. Jeff Kemp could
get a call soon; but rookie Kelly Stouffer, the
Cardinals' '87 top pick, is the Seahawks'
quarterback of the future.

The receivers are excellent, led by future Hall of Famer Steve Largent and improving Darryl Turner. Depth is a question. Top picks Brian Blades and Tommy Kane should help. The line is in good shape, with Ts Ron Mattes, Mike Wilson, and ex-Buc Ron Heller, and Gs Bryan Millard and Edwin Bailey. If C Blair Bush can't make it back, Grant Feasel may get the call. Mike Tice should return at TE.

Defensively, the Seahawks have major problems against the run. NT Joe Nash and DLE Jacob Green were pushed around by offensive linemen last year. The linebacking corps is in great shape, however. LILB Fredd Young is among the NFL's best, and top pick Brian Bosworth showed nice progress as a rookie. Bruce Sholtz should return on the outside left, with Greg Gaines on the outside right. There's good depth here, with perhaps one or two extra LBs available for a trade for a lineman.

A serious kidney ailment will probably end SS Kenny Easley's four-time All-Pro career. Eugene Robinson returns at free safety, with CBs Terry Taylor and much-improved Patrick Hunter back.

The special teams can be excellent. P Ruben Rodriguez did a great job late last season, and PK Norm Johnson is fairly consistent.

Given the problems of the other AFC West teams, the Seahawks aren't in bad shape. A consistent quarterback and a renewed ability to stop the run could help Seattle.

AFC West
DENVER BRONCOS
1987 Finish: First
1988 Prediction: Second

John Elway   **Karl Mecklenburg**

Just when you thought the Broncos were ready to become a dominant team, they blew it. Yes, they've been the best in the west. Yes, they've gone to two straight Super Bowls. But the Super XXII blowout loss to the Redskins proved that the Super XXI blowout loss to the Giants was no fluke.

It seems like a repeat of last year. We know Denver has a fine coach in Dan Reeves. We know Denver has a tremendous quarterback in John Elway. We also know that Denver's defense can give up yardage and points in large chunks. And we know that Denver's running game is, at best, ordinary.

The saving grace is that the entire AFC has problems. Elway (224 of 410, 3,198 yards, 19 TDs), though not among the top ten rated passers in the NFL, still finds ways to win. Gary Kubiak can fill in, if necessary. The running game hasn't improved. Sammy Winder (196 for 741 yards) is the best runner, especially with Gerald Wilhite's health in question. A big back for those tough yards close to the end zone is needed.

The receivers are outstanding, led by Vance Johnson (42 for 684, 7 TDs). The line does a good job, especially in protecting Elway. LG Keith Bishop, RG Stefan Humphries, and RT Ken Lanier are set. LT Dave Studdard and C Bill Bryan may give way to No. 2 draftee Gerald Perry and to Mike Freeman.

The defensive line is just so-so. DRE Rulon Jones is first-rate. Top pick Ted Gregory will battle Greg Kragen at NT, with Andre Townsend back at DLE.

You can't do much better than Denver's inside linebacker combo of Karl Mecklenburg and Ricky Hunley. Mecklenburg is a killer. Outside, Jim Ryan is 31 and beginning to slip. Michael Brooks is ready to step in. LOLB Simon Fletcher is okay.

The secondary has major problems. LCB Mark Haynes is unhappy (as Giant fans will remember). He could be traded. SS Dennis Smith, one of the NFL's best, and FS Tony Lilly should return inside. Randy Robbins might be ready to step in. Steve Wilson should return at RCB. Reeves will have to decide what to do with Mike Harden.

Another Super Bowl trip? It's possible. Third in the division? That's possible, too.

AFC West
LOS ANGELES RAIDERS
1987 Finish: Fourth
1988 Prediction: Third

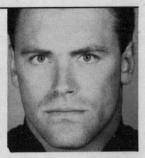

Stacey Toran   **Howie Long**

For the first time since Al Davis arrived in Oakland 25 years ago, the Raiders will start the season with a coach who is not "a Raider guy." Still, most NFL folks think that Mike Shanahan, formerly of the hated Broncos, has a fine offensive mind that could help turn the Raiders around.

If he has a quarterback, that is. The Raiders finished last season with Mark Wilson back at the helm. His 84.6 passing rating was far better than Rusty Hilger's 55.8. Hilger, everyone was led to believe, was the Raiders' QB of the future. At one point early last year, it looked like Redskin Doug Williams was headed to the Raiders. So the hunt for the QB of today continues.

The running game would be in better shape if Bo Jackson doesn't hit major-league curve balls. He'll be a midseason addition again. That leaves the work to Marcus Allen (200 for 754 yards, 51 catches for 410 yards). Jackson averaged 6.8 yards (81 for 554) a year ago. Naval officer Napoleon McCallum may be back.

TE Todd Christensen (47 catches for 663 yards) remains one of the game's top possession receivers. WR James Lofton (41 for 880) was an excellent pickup. He'll rejoin Jessie Hester. The Raiders will look for depth here and on the front line. There should be improvement from tackles Brian Holloway and John Clay, guards Bill Lewis and Dean Miraldi, and center Don Mosebar. It's a young group with potential.

The defense is an aging group. Still, DLE Howie Long remains an All-Pro type, along with NT Bill Pickel. Draftee Scott Davis will help.

Age really begins to show with the linebackers. Linden King and Rod Martin are on the outside with rock-hard Matt Millen and experienced Jerry Robinson inside.

Vann McElroy and Stacey Toran were easily among the best safety pairs in the league. Mike Haynes, Lionel Washington, and Sam Seale will likely battle at CB.

Stan Talley (40.7) didn't make anyone forget long-time Raider punter Ray Guy. But they didn't miss him as much as they thought they would. Chris Bahr is a reliable kicker with fair range. Heisman winner Tim Brown is an excellent kick-returner. Penalties hurt L.A. special teams.

AFC West
SAN DIEGO CHARGERS
1987 Finish: Third
1988 Prediction: Fourth

Billy Ray Smith   **Don Macek**

Since they first entered the NFL in 1970, the Chargers were an offensive team that suffered on defense. Today, for the first time, those roles are reversed. San Diego's defense, despite a late-season slump, became one of the AFC's better units. The offense, despite good pass-run balance, has many question marks.

The retirement of 16-year veteran Dan Fouts leaves a big gap. He finished second all-time in completions (3,297) and yards (43,040). To fill his shoes, the Chargers traded for Pittsburgh failure Mark Malone to join Mike Kelley and Mark Vlasic. None is a Fouts.

The receiving department has problems, too. Ten-year vet Wes Chandler (39 catches) is no longer a deep threat. Lionel James may be a couple of inches too short and a couple of steps too slow. Speedy top pick Anthony Miller may be the deep threat. San Diego may have more quality tight ends than anyone — Kellen Winslow, Eric Sievers, and Pete Holohan. The running game is in fair shape with all-purpose man Gary Anderson, Curtis Adams, and Tim Spencer. Ex-Ram Barry Redden could help.

Up front, LT Jim Lachey and C Don Macek are the leaders. The guards, Dennis McKnight and James FitzPatrick (who overcame preseason knee woes), should be back with right tackles Gary Kowalski and Broderick Thompson.

The Charger defense racked up 45 sacks, seventh in the NFL. Ends Lee Williams and Joe Phillips are coming off fine seasons, with Chuck Ehin and Mike Charles ready to battle for the NT job again. A healthy Leslie O'Neal would help.

The addition of ex-Brown Chip Banks helped the entire linebacking corps. With Banks and San Diego MVP Billy Ray Smith on the outside, the team is set. Gary Plummer and Thomas Benson aren't nearly as good inside.

San Diego's pass defense was fourth in the NFL, which makes the secondary seem better than it is. Still, Al Saunders isn't unhappy with corners Elvis Patterson and Gill Byrd, and safeties Martin Bayless and Vencie Glenn.

Despite some problems, the loss of Fouts at quarterback is by far the biggest.

AFC West
KANSAS CITY CHIEFS
1987 Finish: Fifth
1988 Prediction: Fifth

Deron Cherry   **Christian Okoye**

A 1986 play-off team and a 1987 last-place team (4–11). That's the Kansas City Chiefs. The real story? Somewhere in between. There is hope on offense, problems on defense. In short, coach Frank Gansz needs help.

With Todd Blackledge off to Pittsburgh, the quarterback position belongs to Bill Kenney, if he can keep it. Well-traveled Steve DeBerg arrives from Tampa Bay as the backup, casting his eyes on the starting job. Frank Seurer appears to be Gansz's candidate for QB of the future.

Newcomers Christian Okoye and Paul Palmer helped the rushing game. Okoye was Kaycee's rookie of the year for his 660 yards. Palmer was superb on special teams. The youngsters made a major impact on Herman Heard (466 yards), who had his best season.

WR Carlos Carson is one of the league's top deep threats. His 1,044 yards made up 28% of the Chiefs' total yardage. Stephone Paige is adequate on the other side. The Chiefs' have a major problem at tight end.

On the line, there's talent, size, and potential. That's better than many teams have. Tackles Irv Eatman and John Alt, and guards Mark Adickes and Brian Jozwiak were all high draft picks. Tom Baugh should be back at center.

The switch to a 4–3 defense didn't work for the Chiefs. Led by outstanding tackle Bill Maas, the front group is fair. DE Mike Bell is fine, but Art Still has seen better days. Top pick Neil Smith may fit.

Kaycee needs a killer linebacker to join Dino Hackett, a fine inside 'backer. Tim Cofield should improve with experience.

One of the league's top secondaries still contributed to the league's worst defensive performances. Most coaches would gladly swap with Gansz who has safeties Deron Cherry and Lloyd Burruss, and corners Albert Lewis and Kevin Ross. A little more depth would help here, especially with Mark Robinson traded.

Some folks in Kansas City were unhappy with punter Kelly Goodburn (40.9), and the Chiefs could use some help for returner Paul Palmer. PK Nick Lowery seems fairly certain to hold onto his job.

A turnaround in Kaycee? Not likely.

Human-scoring-machine Jerry Rice scored
22 TDs on 65 catches for San Fran in '87.

National
Football
Conference
Team Previews

NFC East
NEW YORK GIANTS
1987 Finish: Fifth
1988 Prediction: First

Phil Simms   **Lawrence Taylor**

There are lots of reasons why the Giants
became the seventh straight Super Bowl
champs who failed to repeat. There are no
real explanations why they became the first
Super champs who sank to last place.

Try this: In four of the nonstrike Giants'
six losses, they blew fourth-quarter leads.
That's how last-place teams play.

They won't play like that again. There's
too much talent. QB Phil Simms (163 for 282,
2,230 yards, 17 TDs) remains one of the best.
Though there's some grumbling about little
RB Joe Morris (658 yards), he should be
back, along with George Adams, power-
blocker Maurice Carthon, and Lee Rouson.

TE Mark Bavaro (55 catches, 867 yards)
is the game's best — catching and blocking.
A healthy Lionel Manuel should help young

receivers Stephen Baker, Mark Ingram, and Odessa Turner. Phil McConkey, a favorite of coach Bill Parcells, is questionable.

Up front, there will be changes. LT Brad Benson retired, creating even more problems for the troubled offensive line. William Roberts, last year's RT, will return to LT, replacing Benson. If Karl Nelson recovers from Hodgkin's disease, he'll be back at RT. If not, Doug Riesenberg gets the call. LG Bill Ard and C Bart Oates are set, with Damian Johnson pushing RG Chris Godfrey. Top draftees Eric Moore and John Elliott will get long looks.

The Giants have happy problems on defense. Eric Dorsey will push George Martin at LDE, with Jim Burt and Erik Howard battling at NT. Leonard Marshall is the RE.

Linebacking is super. No one — maybe ever — has enjoyed a pair of outside linebackers like Lawrence Taylor and Carl Banks. They're awesome. Vet Harry Carson may get pressure from Gary Reasons and Pepper Johnson on the inside.

The secondary is the weak link on defense. Safeties Kenny Hill and Terry Kinard will both be returning from surgery. Look for Greg Lasker and Adrian White to push Hill at strong safety. Mark Collins and Perry Williams should return at the corners.

For the Giants to return to the top of the NFC East, they will have to (1) stay healthy, (2) avoid fourth-quarter collapses, and (3) reduce their penalties.

NFC East
WASHINGTON REDSKINS
1987 Finish: First
1988 Prediction: Second

Joe Jacoby   **Darrell Green**

Pity poor Joe Gibbs. Considered the new "genius" of pro football, the chief Redskin will be faced with all sorts of difficult decisions as the '88 season starts. Every coach in the NFL would gladly swap problems with him.

There's no question that Jay Schroeder is the Skins' quarterback of the future. But after Doug Williams's play-off and Super Bowl wonders, how can Gibbs (and fans) argue with him. Hero Williams has the job until he loses it.

RB Kelvin Bryant has never lived up to his USFL promise. And now Timmy Smith is coming off a super Super Bowl (204 yards). Another delicious problem for Gibbs.

Receiving is in great shape. A healthy Art Monk will do battle with his replacement,

Ricky Sanders, and fleet Gary Clark. Up front, Jeff Bostic seems to be back, battling with vet Russ Grimm at center. The rest of the returning Hogs are aging, a future problem (not delicious) for Gibbs. Look for Joe Jacoby (LT), Raleigh McKenzie (LG), R.C. Thielemann (RG), and Mark May (RT) to hang in for another year.

Ex-Bear LB Wilber Marshall, the new six-million-dollar man, will certainly anchor an improved Skin defense that features one of the best secondary groups in the league. Alvin Walton and Todd Bowles are, possibly, the best pair of safeties. CB Barry Wilburn led the NFL in interceptions and should be matched again with speedy Darrell Green. If Gibbs has a complaint about the secondary, it's their tendency to give up lots of air mileage. Up front, oft-angry Dexter Manley should be even more effective at RDE with the addition of Marshall. LDT Dave Butz's days are numbered, but Charles Mann and Darryl Grant should be set. There will be plenty of movement at the linebacker positions, where Marshall joins Mel Kaufman, Neal Olkewicz, and Monte Coleman.

If the Skins have any problems, it's on special teams. Gibbs added a new special teams coach, but still faces problems with his placekicker. Ali Haji-Sheikh replaced Jess Atkinson after one game last year. They'll battle top pick Chip Lohmiller for the position this year. A long-snapper could help here, too.

NFC East
PHILADELPHIA EAGLES
1987 Finish: Fourth
1988 Prediction: Third

Randall Cunningham   **Mike Quick**

Strange doings in the City of Brotherly
Love. With the NFL's top QB sacker, Reggie
White, doing his thing, the Eagles still finished last in the NFC in pass defense. (The
strike team didn't help.) And with Randall
Cunningham, one of the most exciting and
mobile quarterbacks in the NFL, the Eagles
allowed sacks almost as fast as White
could make them.

In only 12 games, All-Pro DE Reggie
White missed the 16-game sack record by
only one. In fact, the Eagles had one of the
most fearsome pass-rushes in the league.
DT Jerome Brown could be brilliant, if his
on-again off-again elbow injury heals. By
the end of the '87 season, rookie Bryon
Evans was set at MLB, where he should
replace Mike Reichenbach for good. Watch

for Mike Pitts to step in for Ken Clarke at left defensive tackle and Dwayne Jiles to replace Garry Cobb at OLB. Coach Buddy Ryan is beginning to shape the defense in the image he brought from Chicago.

The secondary is led by hard-hitting Roynell Young at the corner and strong safety Andre Waters. An overall improvement by the defense, particularly against the run, will vault the Eagles toward the top. Rookie CB Eric Allen will help.

On offense, Cunningham makes things happen. He threw for 2,786 yards and 23 TDs last year. Most of the 50 nonstrike sacks put Cunningham on his back. Even worse, Cunningham was also the Eagles' leading rusher (505 yards, 6.6 average).

Cunningham's exciting style led to all sorts of big plays, with quick Mike Quick at wide receiver usually at the other end. Top draftee TE Keith Jackson could start right away. The running game, led by Keith Byars and Anthony Toney, was slightly improved in '87, but still has a way to go. An improved offensive line would help enormously. The Eagles were one of the few NFL teams that had the same starting line in the first and last games last year.

Look for changes in the special teams. PK Paul McFadden has now suffered through two straight off-years, hitting on only 61.5% of his FG tries last year. Punter John Teltschik slipped from 41.6 yards per punt as a rookie to only 38.2. Kick returns? The Eagles were last in that department.

NFC East
DALLAS COWBOYS
1987 Finish: Third
1988 Prediction: Fourth

Herschel Walker   **Everson Walls**

Whatever happened to America's team? They're not even Texas's team anymore. Houston made the NFL play-offs in '87; Dallas went 7–8. The offensive line is too young, the defensive line is too old, and the owner is jumping on coach Tom Landry.

A Cowboy comeback — unlikely in '88 — hinges on Herschel Walker, the team's do-everything back. He became the first NFL player to total more than 700 yards rushing (891) and receiving (715) twice in his career. With Tony Dorsett looking to get out at age 34, Walker will again team with FB Timmy Newsome.

Landry figures to open the season with Steve Pelluer at QB. Pelluer led the team to season-ending victories over the Rams and Cardinals, and has thrown 94 passes without an interception. Vet Danny White (700 yards in his last two starts) will be ready to back up, with Kevin Sweeney a possible QB of the future.

Mike Sherrard, projected as the Cowboys' top receiver a year ago before suffering a badly broken leg, broke it again last spring while running on the beach. Dallas's top pick, Michael Irvin, must be ready now. Ten-year vet Mike Renfro is set, along with Rod Barksdale, Kelvin Edwards, and Kelvin Martin. TE Doug Cosbie is solid.

Up front, only C Tom Rafferty has much NFL experience. Tackles Daryle Smith and 310-pound Kevin Gogan, and guards Crawford Ker and 315-pound Nate Newton have only seven years of experience between them. Injured LT Mark Tuinei and LG Glen Titensor could well regain their old starting positions.

Age has overtaken the defensive line where Too Tall Jones (10 sacks) still has something left. LT Randy White may be sliding downhill, with Kevin Brooks and Danny Noonan ready to take over at the tackles. RE Jim Jeffcoat is sound.

Recovery from a trio of broken legs could restore the Cowboy linebackers, MVP Eugene Lockhart, Mike Hegman, and Jesse Penn. Ron Burton and Steve DeOssie will be back.

CBs Ron Francis and Everson Walls are just fine, thank you. At safety, Vince Albritton and Victor Scott will challenge Bill Bates and Michael Downs.

NFC East
PHOENIX CARDINALS
1987 Finish: Second
1988 Prediction: Fifth

Stump Mitchell   **Neil Lomax**

Arizona fans: Did you know that in 28 seasons in St. Louis, the Cards never played a play-off game at home and never won a play-off game anywhere?

Despite the fact that the Cards came within a final-game win (they lost to Dallas) of making the '87 play-offs, they're not as likely to come that close this year. The offense is fair (depending upon which Neil Lomax shows up in Phoenix), but the defense is awful. And NFL champions win with defense.

Lomax, supposedly through before '87, put in a Pro Bowl year (275 for 463, 3,387 yards, 24 TDs). He is blessed with top receivers, including long-time star Roy Green and surprising 12-year man J.T. Smith. Waived by Kansas City in '85, Smith showed up in St. Louis where he caught 171 passes the last two years. His 91 catches last year led the league. TE Robert Awalt won at least one Rookie of the Year award last year. It's a good crew.

RBs Stump Mitchell and Earl Ferrell provided enough balance for the passing game. Mitchell is the Cards' all-time combined yardage leader (10,277).

LT Luis Sharpe anchors a fine offensive line that features LG Todd Peat, C Derek Kennard, RG Lance Smith, and RT Tootie Robbins. Former starter Joe Bostic should be a great backup guard.

The defense was 12th (among 14) in the NFC against the run and 13th against the pass. Sad. Ends David Galloway and Freddie Joe Nunn contain pretty well, with Bob Clasby and Steve Alvord inside doing okay (no better) against the run. But the pass-rush is barely so-so. Changes could also come at linebacker where hard-hitting Niko Noga roams the middle. E.J. Junior and Anthony Bell could return on the outside. Top pick Ken Harvey could win a spot. The LBs caused only five turnovers in '87.

SS Leonard Smith paces the defensive backfield. He should be a Pro Bowler every year. But the Cards intercepted only 14 passes last year and allowed 30 TD passes. That says something about the group of Smith, FS Lonnie Young, CB Carl Carter, and CB Cedric Mack.

Vai Sikahema, one of the NFL's top kick-returners, heads the special teams.

NFC Central
CHICAGO BEARS
1987 Finish: First
1988 Prediction: First

Neal Anderson   **Richard Dent**

The Minnesota Vikings are licking their chops. After reaching the NFC championship game, the Vikes are now casting eyes on the NFC Central title that Chicago has owned for years.

It shouldn't happen. Even without retired safety Gary Fencik, retired all-timer Walter Payton, and departed ILB Wilber Marshall, the Bears still have enough talent to win. They can, if they don't beat themselves.

There's plenty of talent in the Windy City. But the Bears always seem to be sniping — at each other, at their coaches, at everyone. Coach Mike Ditka says the complainers have to go. That will leave him pretty lonely.

QB Jim McMahon will be ready to go in '88, with Neal Anderson, the team's leading rusher (586 yards on 129 carries) and receiver (47 for 467 yards), right behind him in the backfield. Top pick Brad Muster will see action.

Chicago is loaded with receivers. Ron Morris started as a rookie (20 for 379 yards) opposite Willie Gault (705 yards and 7 TDs). Extra receiver Dennis McKinnon returned two punts for TDs in '87.

On the offensive line, C Jay Hilgenberg is coming off elbow surgery. LT Jim Covert is rock-solid. The rest of the line has problems. Look for challenges to LG Mark Bortz, RG Tom Thayer, and RT Keith Van Horne.

The loss of Marshall hurts the defense where LLB Otis Wilson is already unhappy. MLB Mike Singletary is the team leader. Up front, there's no one better than tackle Steve McMichael, an All-Pro. LE Dan Hampton is outstanding, but RT Fridge Perry may eat his way out of a starting spot.

The secondary, with Fencik gone, is in some trouble. Cornerbacks Vestee Jackson and Mike Richardson are the returning starters, but neither is a world-beater. There could be a change here. Free safety Dave Duerson is back from another Pro Bowl season.

A healthy McMahon is a key. Jim Harbaugh needs more experience, and Mike Tomczak will never make it. There's enough talent for a run at Super Bowl XXIII. But there's also enough trouble for the team to blow its leadership in the NFC Central.

NFC Central
MINNESOTA VIKINGS
1987 Finish: Second
1988 Prediction: Second

D.J. Dozier   **Tommy Kramer**

Streaks don't win championships. Consistency wins championships. The '87 Vikings were a streak team. Coach Jerry Burns's 1988 objective is to develop a consistent team.

He has the tools to do it. He has good quarterbacking, perhaps too much of it. He has excellent team speed. And he has a team that taught itself it could win with the best in the '87–'88 play-offs. Not bad for starters.

Speaking of starters, Burns will have to decide between QBs Tommy Kramer and Wade Wilson. Oft-injured Kramer (40 for 81) had to give way to backup Wilson (140 for 264, 2,106 yards, 14 TDs), who was in and out. Wilson was also the Vikes' third-leading rusher (263 yards), behind Darrin Nelson (131 for 642) and Alfred Anderson (319).

Burns will have to figure a way to get the ball into the hands of Anthony (A.C.) Carter. The former Michigan flash averaged a league-leading 24.3 yards per catch, but on only 38 receptions. Flanker Leo Lewis and backup Hassan Jones join Carter, with tough Steve Jordan back at TE.

The front five is solid, led by tackles Gary Zimmerman (an All-Pro) and Tim Irwin. David Huffman and Greg Koch will battle with top pick Randall McDaniel and Terry Tausch at guard. Tausch returns from the IR (ankle). Kirk Lowdermilk is the center.

The Vikes' linebacking needs help. David Howard and Jesse Solomon could return outside with Scott Studwell at MLB.

Up front, tough RT Keith Millard exerts tons of pressure on the inside, making it easier for RE Chris Doleman to crash the opponents' backfield. Add LE Doug Martin and young LT Henry Thomas and you have a first-rate unit.

All-Pro Joey Browner, one of the game's hardest hitters, anchors the secondary from his strong safety spot. John Harris joins him at free safety, with Issiac Holt and Carl Lee seemingly set at the corners. Three of Minny's first six draft picks were DBs.

Burns will have to find a reliable punter to really soar in '88. But with youngsters like CB Reggie Rutland, S Neal Guggemos, and RBs D.J. Dozier and Rick Fenney ready to make their breaks, the Vikings will battle the Bears down to the wire.

NFC Central
TAMPA BAY BUCCANEERS
1987 Finish: Fourth
1988 Prediction: Third

Vinny Testaverde

Scot Brantley

If coach Ray Perkins built buildings instead of football teams, he'd probably start with office complexes. Nothing simple for the former N.Y. Giant and Alabama U. boss. His job is underway, but the "building" still has lots of "floors" to go.

With Steve DeBerg off to Kansas City, the QB job belongs to Vinny Testaverde. Though the ex-Miami star went 0–4 in four late-season starts, he showed flashes of future greatness.

The running game is a key for the Bucs. The defense spent '87 learning to stop it. The offense, however, must still learn how to make it go. FB James Wilder led the team with 488 yards (the 6th straight year he has topped Tampa rushers), but his '88 status is in question. There isn't much at tailback, where Jeff Smith, Cliff Austin, and Bobby Howard can't seem to cut it.

For Testaverde to succeed, last year's young receivers must improve. WRs Mark Carrier and Bruce Hill combined for 49 catches. Ron Hall could be Tampa's TE of the future. Vets Gerald Carter, Phil Freeman, and Calvin Magee will press them.

Up front, the key is better run-blocking. C Randy Grimes is solid. The rest of the line is full of question marks. Guards Rick Mallory and George Yarno will return, unless Dan Turk can unseat one. A healthy Rob Taylor could return at LT, with Mark Cooper, J.D. Maarleveld, and top pick Paul Gruber battling for a starting spot.

The Bucs' defense went from 28th in the NFL to 16th in '87, a marked improvement. Led by DE Ron Holmes, the line nearly doubled its sack total (9½ to 18). John Cannon will be back at left end, with Mike Stensrud hoping to hold off Dan Sileo and Curt Jarvis at nose tackle.

ILB Ervin Randle (108 tackles) is becoming one of the league's best, along with Jeff Davis and Scot Brantley on the inside and Chris Washington on the outside.

Count on young Ricky Reynolds and Rod Jones to return at the corners. You can't count on anyone at safety, where no one really stuck out last year.

Kick-returner Bobby Futrell is solid, though not spectacular, and PK Donald Igwebuike is accurate. With P Frank Garcia gone, the special teams may be rebuilt.

71

NFC Central
GREEN BAY PACKERS
1987 Finish: Third
1988 Prediction: Fourth

Randy Wright   **Mark Lee**

Lindy Infante has a problem. The Packers' new head coach takes over a program that has had only four winning seasons in 20 years. There are players with all sorts of troubles. And there are positions with all sorts of player troubles. Still, the Packers' bosses figure the team is ready to win. So Infante will have to win — and soon.

First, there's the QB derby. Infante, an offensive expert, will likely settle on one QB. It could be Don Majkowski, called "the QB of the future" by ex-coach Forrest Gregg. It could be Randy Wright, the man with experience. Even ex-BYU star Robbie Bosco could get a shot.

The running game is in good shape with the combo of Brent Fullwood and Kenneth Davis. Davis (413) yards led the Pack a year ago. Rookie Keith Woodside could help.

The rest of the offensive crew is, well, okay. WR Phil Epps is No. 10 on the all-time Green Bay list with 180 catches, 34 last year. Walter Stanley, Frankie Neal, and top pick Sterling Sharpe should be ready to go. Infante will have to get his running backs into the passing game.

On the line, tackles Ken Ruettgers (the Pack's offensive MVP) and Keith Uecker (voted Green Bay's most courageous player) anchor the group. Guards Rich Moran and Ron Hallstrom, and center Mark Cannon could be back.

The defense is in somewhat better shape. Linebacking is in good hands, with Tim Harris on the right outside, opposite veteran John Anderson. Brian Noble is solid on the inside, along with Johnny Holland.

The defensive line needs lots of work. Last year's trio of ends (Alphonso Carreker, Jerry Boyarsky, and Robert Brown) didn't get it done in '87. Things are a little more settled in the Packer secondary where Mark Lee and Dave Brown should return on the corners, and Mark Murphy and Ken Stills look set at safety.

PK Max Zendejas showed up with the Packers' replacement team, then stayed as the regular kicker. Don Bracken is the returning punter.

The '87 Packers played just about everyone tough. Tough, however, does not spell victory. Green Bay is more than a couple of players away.

NFC Central
DETROIT LIONS
1987 Finish: Fifth
1988 Prediction: Fifth

Chuck Long   Jimmy Williams

Last time the Lions won a play-off game? It was the NFL title match in 1957! (Ask your grandparents about Bobby Layne and Buddy Parker.) Their next play-off win still seems years away.

Be patient with QB Chuck Long. He has a few things to learn, but he's getting better. His 232 completions in 417 attempts for 2,598 yards put him right up with all-time Detroit QBs. (He was sacked only 17 times in 12 games, which helped.)

One of his biggest problems was a lack of good receivers. No problem with WR Pete Mandley (58 receptions). But the rest of the cast wasn't much. Coach Darryl Rogers (who will start the season, at least) figures that TE David Hill could help. Second-year man Gary Lee could improve.

If the James gang is healthy, Detroit could make some strides in '88. That's RB Garry James and FB James Jones. They gained 1,591 yards in 1986, then were hit hard by injuries in '87 and slipped to only 612 yards.

Up front, the offensive line is pretty fair, led by Ts Lomas Brown and Harvey Salem. Scott Barrows, Steve Mott, and Kevin Glover finished '87 in the middle, where '87 rookie Joe Milinichik and returners from injury could help.

Though there's some hope on offense, there's much less on defense. Detroit allowed 30 or more points seven times in '87 — and lost every time. Rogers still looks to solid citizens in several spots. LOLB Jimmy Williams is super against the run and knows what to do against the pass, especially in nickel coverage. Strong safety James Griffin is the leading light in a secondary that gave up passing yards in huge chunks (3,558) last year. Top draftee S Bennie Blades has lots of talent.

Rogers is pleased with the progress of '87 rookies ILB Dennis Gibson and NT Jerry Ball, who started every game last season. Gibson led the team with 82 tackles. OLB Mike Cofer joins Williams to make Detroit respectable on the outside. Draft pick Chris Spielman is a future star.

Despite Pro Bowl punter Jim Arnold and big-hitting Paul Butcher, Detroit special teams are in trouble, too. PK Eddie Murray was in and out (mostly out) on a unit that will be well shaken in '88.

NEW ORLEANS SAINTS
1987 Finish: Second
1988 Prediction: First

Bobby Hebert   **Rueben Mayes**

New Orleans is a town that likes to party.
(Super Bowl, Sugar Bowl, and Mardi Gras
visitors know it for sure.) Now the town is
ready to party for one of its own, the Saints.
Question is, are the Saints as good as their
12–3 record in '87 would seem to show?

The 44–10 loss to Minnesota in the play-
offs helps hammer that question home. The
Saints can certainly run the football. Their
basic defense seems solid. And their special teams are really special. But, for the
one-time Ain'ts to show that 12–3 was no
fluke, they'll have to do more things in '88.

Bobby Hebert (164 for 294, 2,119 yards, 15
TDs) enjoyed the best passer rating of any
Saint QB — ever. No full-time NFL starter
threw fewer interceptions than Hebert (9).
The running game was most effective —

from tackle to tackle. Both Rueben Mayes (917 yards) and Dalton Hilliard (508 yards) were solid. Now there's more power with huge RB (and top pick) Ironhead Heyward. Coach Jim Mora will still have to find some speed for the run to go outside.

The receivers must be improved for the passing game to go. Eric Martin (44 catches) lacks real speed. Mike Jones is a good possession receiver. Lonzell Hill is so-so. Draftee Brett Perriman could help. RG Steve Trapilo was a pleasant surprise as a rookie, but LT Jim Dombrowski is still a question mark. A healthy Steve Korte may move to LG, with Joel Hilgenberg at C. Stan Brock returns at RT, but where will Brad Edelman play after a Pro Bowl year?

The defensive line is fairly good — and could get better if James Geathers and Shawn Knight earn their money. Bruce Clark, Tony Elliott, and Jim Wilks are solid.

Mora is pleased with his linebackers, led by Pro Bowler Rickey Jackson. A couple of former USFL stars, Sam Mills and Vaughan Johnson, performed well for former USFL coach Mora. Pat Swilling is improving.

The secondary, however, is a problem area. Cornerbacks Dave Waymer and Van Jakes have been inconsistent. Troubled Reggie Sutton could help here. SS Gene Atkins will be challenged by former starter Antonio Gibson. Toi Cook will likely be the free safety.

Special teams are ably headed by PK Morten Andersen, the Saints' MVP.

NFC West
SAN FRANCISCO 49ERS
1987 Finish: First
1988 Prediction: Second

Roger Craig   **Joe Montana**

The Niners are at the crossroads. An early Super Bowl favorite when the '87 play-offs began, San Francisco was smashed by Minnesota. QB Joe Montana was yanked early in favor of Steve Young. Montana has not produced a TD in SF's last three post-season outings. And then the questions began.

Despite an All-Pro season, Montana (266 for 398, 3,054 yards, 31 TDs) was the subject of off-season trade rumors. Ex-USFL star Young had 10 TDs on only 37 completions in '87 and may be ready to lead an NFL contender. There are lots of questions about the Niners' offensive line. OT Keith Fahnhorst is prepping for his 15th NFL season, C Randy Cross for his 13th, and backup C Fred Quillan for his 11th. LT

Bubba Paris is probably in good shape, despite an injury suffered in the New Orleans game last year. OG Paul McIntyre was also sidelined. Jesse Sapolu is ready to start, and there's great hope for young Harris Barton and Bruce Collie.

There's no question about receivers. Jerry Rice (65 for 1,078 yards and 22 TDs) is the best there is. Ex-Raider Dokie Williams, Dwight Clark, and Mike Wilson provide great depth. TE is capably handled by Mike Frank and Ron Heller. Roger Craig (815 yards rushing, 492 yards on 66 catches) heads the running game, with able support from Joe Cribbs and Tom Rathman.

On defense, LB Keena Turner had major knee surgery and may be through. That only makes things worse for a defense that was the weakest part of the Niners' game a year ago. San Francisco had trouble stopping opposing runners, though the secondary, led by All-Pro safety Ronnie Lott, did well against the pass.

Jeff Stover and Pete Kugler on the left side, Michael Carter in the middle, and Dwaine Board on the right will take most of the heat for the poor rush defense. Draftee Daniel Stubs will help. Milt McColl will probably start at the left outside LB spot, joining Mike Walter at RILB. The other positions may be up for grabs.

LCB Tim McKyer seems set to join FS Lott in the secondary. Jeff Fuller and Carlton Williamson will battle for the SS spot with Don Griffin leading the way at RCB.

NFC West
LOS ANGELES RAMS
1987 Finish: Third
1988 Prediction: Third

Jerry Gray   **Jim Everett**

Credit coach John Robinson. The '87 Rams were truly Team Trouble. Yet the vet field boss held things together pretty well. True, the Rams finished 6–9 after a 48–0 loss to San Francisco. It could have been worse.

Robinson and his staff have plenty of work to do for '88, but they'll be helped by the draft picks they've earned for Eric Dickerson and others.

The jury is still out on QB Jim Everett. He showed some signs of becoming a top pro passer last year (162 for 302, 2,064 yards, only 10 TDs). He'll have to do it every week for the Rams to succeed.

Can Charles White do it again? Taking over for the traded Dickerson, White rushed for a league-leading 1,374 yards, just four fewer than his previous seven NFL seasons combined. The Rams hope top draftee Gaston Green can be his running mate.

WR Henry Ellard had trouble catching the ball last season. And running mate Ron Brown quit to resume his Olympic track career. Rookie Aaron Cox could be the answer. TE David Hill was cut last winter. The front five is in transition. RG Dennis Harrah retired. C Doug Smith is starting his 11th season, and RT Jackie Slater his 13th. LG Tom Newberry is a future All-Pro, and LT Irv Pankey can still play.

The biggest question marks on defense rest with the secondary. RCB LeRoy Irvin was unhappy for most of '87. While FS Nolan Cromwell is still solid, age is beginning to show. Jerry Gray at LCB seems set, with young Michael Stewart probably ready at SS.

Comeback star RILB Jim Collins returned from a 1986 shoulder injury (he missed the entire season) to lead the Ram tacklers with 98. No one else had more than 62. The rest of the unit (LOLB Mel Owens, LILB Carl Ekern, and ROLB Mike Wilcher) is a veteran crew.

Up front, DE Gary Jeter will likely be gone. The front three (LE Doug Reed, NT Greg Meisner, and RE Shawn Miller) will be ready to go, with help from ends Fred Stokes and Kevin Greene.

Kickers Mike Lansford (placements) and Dale Hatcher (punts) key the Rams' special teams. The coverage units do an excellent job.

NFC West
ATLANTA FALCONS
1987 Finish: Fourth
1988 Prediction: Fourth

Bill Curry

Bill Fralic

Things have to get better in Atlanta. They simply cannot get worse. About the only statistical group Atlanta dominated last season was "lasts." They were last in points scored (205); worst in points allowed (436); and at the bottom in first downs, rushing attempts and yards, defense, rushing yards and TDs allowed, and total TDs allowed. Their defense turned in only 17 sacks, four fewer than Philadelphia's Reggie White by himself.

Whew! The good news, if any, starts with the signing of Auburn LB Aundray Bruce as the NFL's top draft pick. He should help the pass-rush.

The offense isn't much. Gerald Riggs knows how to run the football (203 carries for 875 yards). Kenny Flowers, John Settle, and Sylvester Stamps will lead a crowd looking to join Riggs in the backfield. Chris Miller, the 1987 No. 1 draft pick, started two games last year and figures to get the first shot in '88. If he can't make it, look for Scott Campbell to return.

The Falcon receivers are all speedy, led by Floyd Dixon, Stacey Bailey, and Aubrey Matthews. They need a QB who can get the ball to them. A healthy Ken Whisenhunt and rookie Alex Higdon will help at TE.

The line is G Bill Fralic and a bunch of other guys. Fralic is as good as they come. A healthy Bret Miller will fill the bill at one tackle spot.

If the Falcon defense has any strengths, they're up front. Ends Mike Gann and Rick Bryan work with nose man Tony Casillas. They'll be even more effective if Aundray Bruce and Marcus Cotton turn out to be the linebackers coach Marion Campbell thinks they can be. The returning LBs — Tim Green, Joe Costello, John Rade, and Joel Williams (from left to right) — just didn't get the job done a year ago.

There will also be changes in a secondary that allowed yardage by the chunk in '87. Although Campbell planned to go to camp with a veteran group including corners Bobby Butler and Scott Case and safeties Robert Moore and Tim Gordon, bet there will be plenty of changes.

League-leading punter Rick Donnelly will be back along with the top kickoff-returner Sylvester Stamps.

Huge Bruce Smith leads an upgraded Bill
defense toward the top of the AFC East.

1988
NFL
Draft List

The following abbreviations are used to identify the players' positions:

OFFENSE:
T = tackle; G = guard; C = center;
QB = quarterback; RB = running back;
WR = wide receiver; TE = tight end.

DEFENSE:
DE = defensive end;
DT = defensive tackle; LB = linebacker;
DB = defensive back.

SPECIAL TEAMS:
P = punter; K = placekicker.

The number preceding the player's name indicates the overall position in which he was drafted.

Atlanta Falcons
1. Aundray Bruce, LB, Auburn; 28. Marcus Cotton, LB, USC; 56. Alex Higdon, TE, Ohio St.; 110. Charles Dimry, DB, Nevada-Las Vegas; 128. George Thomas, WR, Nevada-Las Vegas; 140. Houston Hoover, G, Jackson St.; 166. Michael Haynes, WR, No. Arizona; 194. Phillip Brown, LB, Alabama; 222. James Primus, RB, UCLA; 250. Stan Clayton, T, Penn St.; 278. James Milling, WR, Maryland; 306. Carter Wiley, DB, Virginia Tech.

Buffalo Bills

40. Thurman Thomas, RB, Oklahoma St.; 66. Bernard Ford, WR, Central Florida; 123. Zeke Gadson, DB, Pitt; 135. Kirk Roach, K, W. Carolina; 150. Dan Murray, LB, E. Stroudsburg (PA); 177. Tim Borcky, T, Memphis St.; 184. Bo Wright, RB, Alabama; 204. John Hagy, DB, Texas; 213. Jeff Wright, DT, Central Missouri St.; 235. Carlton Bailey, DT, No. Carolina; 262. Martin Mayhew, DB, Florida St.; 289. Pete Curkendall, DT, Penn St.; 309. John Driscoll, T, New Hampshire; 316. Tom Erlandson, LB, Washington.

Chicago Bears

23. Brad Muster, RB, Stanford; 27. Wendell Davis, WR, LSU; 51. Dante Jones, LB, Oklahoma; 78. Ralph Jarvis, DE, Temple; 105. Jim Thornton, TE, Cal. St.-Fullerton; 133. Troy Johnson, LB, Oklahoma; 161. Lemuel Stinson, DB, Texas Tech; 189. Caesar Rentie, T, Oklahoma; 208. David Tate, DB, Colorado; 217. Harvey Reed, RB, Howard; 245. Rogie Magee, WR, LSU; 273. Joel Porter, G, Baylor; 301. Steve Forch, LB, Nebraska; 329. Greg Clark, LB, Arizona St.

Cincinnati Bengals

5. Rickey Dixon, DB, Oklahoma; 31. Ickey Woods, RB, Nevada-Las Vegas; 57. Kevin Walker, LB, Maryland; 84. David Grant, DT, West Virginia; 114. Herb Wester, T, Iowa; 141. Paul Jetton, G, Texas; 168. Richard Romer, LB, Union (NY); 195. Curtis Maxey, DT, Grambling; 226. Brandy Wells, DB, Notre Dame; 253. Ellis Dilahunt, DB, E. Carolina; 280. Paul Hickert, K, Murray St.; 307. Carl Parker, WR, Vanderbilt.

Cleveland Browns

21. Clifford Charlton, LB, Florida; 50. Michael Dean Perry, DT, Clemson; 77. Van Waiters, LB, Indiana; 104. Anthony Blaylock, DB, Winston-Salem St.; 188. Thane Gash, DB, E. Tennessee St.; 216. J.J. Birden, WR, Oregon; 244. Denny Copeland, DB, E. Kentucky; 272. Brian Washington, DB, Nebraska; 300. Hendley Hawkins, WR, Nebraska; 328. Steve Slayden, QB, Duke.

Dallas Cowboys

11. Michael Irvin, WR, Miami; 41. Ken Norton, LB, UCLA; 67. Mark Hutson, G, Oklahoma; 94. David Widell, T, Boston Col.; 151. Scott Secules, QB, Virginia; 178. Owen Hooven, T, Oregon St.; 205. Mark Higgs, RB, Kentucky; 232. Brian Bedford, WR, California; 263. Billy Owens, DB, Pitt.; 290. Chad Hennings, DT, Air Force; 317. Ben Hummell, LB, UCLA.

Denver Broncos

26. Ted Gregory, DT, Syracuse; 45. Gerald Perry, T, Southern; 79. Kevin Guidry, DB, LSU; 136. Corris Ervin, DB, Central Florida; 174. Pat Kelly, TE, Syracuse; 192. Garry Frank, C, Mississippi St.; 248. Mel Farr, RB, UCLA; 268. Channing Williams, RB, Arizona St.; 304. Richard Calvin, RB, Washington St.; 332. Johnny Carter, DT, Grambling.

Detroit Lions

3. Bennie Blades, DB, Miami; 29. Chris Spielman, LB, Ohio St.; 32. Pat Carter, TE, Florida St.; 58. Ray Roundtree, WR, Penn St.; 85. William White, DB, Ohio St.; 111. Eric Andolsek, G, LSU; 142. Carl Painter, RB, Hampton; 169. Jeff James, WR, Stanford; 198. Gary Hadd, DE, Minnesota; 223. Kip Corrington, DB, Texas A&M; 234. Todd Irvin, T, Mississippi; 254. Paco Craig, WR, UCLA; 281. Danny McCoin, QB, Cincinnati.

Green Bay Packers

7. Sterling Sharpe, WR, South Carolina; 34. Shawn Patterson, DT, Arizona St.; 61. Keith Woodside, RB, Texas A&M; 88. Rollin Putzier, DT, Oregon; 89. Chuck Cecil, DB, Arizona; 116. Darrell Reed, LB, Oklahoma; 144. Nate Hill, DE, Auburn; 172. Gary Richard, DB, Pitt; 200. Patrick Collins, RB, Oklahoma; 228. Neal Wilkinson, TE, James Madison; 256. Bud Keyes, QB, Wisconsin; 312. Scott Bolton, WR, Auburn.

Houston Oilers

22. Lorenzo White, RB, Michigan St.; 48. Quintin Jones, DB, Pitt; 72. Greg Montgomery, P, Michigan St.; 125. Chris Dishman, DB, Purdue; 130. Chris Verhulst, TE, Cal. St.-Chico; 157. Kurt Crain, LB, Auburn; 187. Tracey Eaton, RB, Portland St.; 214. Dave Visene, C, Minnesota-Duluth; 241. David Spradlin, LB, TCU; 271. Marco Johnson, WR, Hawaii; 298. Jethro Franklin, DT, Fresno St.; 325. John Brantley, LB, Georgia.

Indianapolis Colts

76. Chris Chandler, QB, Washington; 102. Michael Ball, DB, Southern; 129. John Baylor, DB, Southern Miss.; 243. Jeff Herrod, LB, Mississippi; 270. O'Brien Alston, LB, Maryland; 297. Donnie Dee, DE, Tulsa; 308. Aatron Kenney, WR, Wisconsin-Stevens Point; 327. Tim Vesling, K, Syracuse.

Kansas City Chiefs

2. Neil Smith, DE, Nebraska; 59. Kevin Porter, DB, Auburn; 96. J.R. Ambrose, WR, Mississippi; 139. James Saxon, RB, San Jose St.; 170. Troy Stedman, LB, Washburn; 197. Alfredo Roberts, TE, Miami; 224. Azizuddin Abdur-Ra'oof, WR, Maryland; 251. Kenny Gamble, RB, Colgate; 282. Danny McManus, QB, Florida St.

Los Angeles Raiders

6. Tim Brown, WR, Notre Dame; 9. Terry McDaniel, DB, Tennessee; 25. Scott Davis, DE, Illinois; 90. Tim Rother, DE, Nebraska; 131. Dennis Price, DB, UCLA; 143. Erwin Grabisna, LB, Case Western; 171. Derrick Crudup, DB, Oklahoma; 199. Michael Alexander, WR, Penn St.; 227. Reggie Ware, RB, Auburn; 229. Scott Tabor, P, California; 255. Newt Harrell, T, W. Texas St.; 283. David Weber, QB, Carroll (WI); 311. Greg Kunkel, G, Kentucky.

Los Angeles Rams

14. Gaston Green, RB, UCLA; 20. Aaron Cox, WR, Arizona St.; 35. Anthony Newman, DB, Oregon; 46. Willie Anderson, WR, UCLA; 47. Fred Strickland, LB, Purdue; 82. Mike Piel, DT, Illinois; 117. Robert Delpino, RB, Missouri; 137. James Washington, DB, UCLA; 147. Keith Jones, RB, Nebraska; 165. Jeff Knapton, DT, Wyoming; 201. Darryl Franklin, WR, Washington; 231. Pat Foster, T, Montana; 258. R.C. Mullin, T, S.W. Louisiana; 333. Jeff Beathard, WR, So. Oregon.

Miami Dolphins

16. Eric Kumerow, DE, Ohio St.; 42. Jarvis Williams, DB, Florida; 73. Ferrell Edmunds, TE, Maryland; 99. Greg Johnson, G, Oklahoma; 125. Rodney Thomas, DB, Brigham Young; 153. Melvin Bratton, RB, Miami; 156. George Cooper, RB, Ohio St.; 180. Kerwin Bell, QB, Florida; 212. Harry Galbreath, G, Tennessee; 220. Louis Cheek, T, Texas A&M; 239. Jeff Cross, DE, Missouri; 266. Artis Jackson, DT, Texas Tech; 293. Tom Kelleher, RB, Holy Cross; 320. Brian Kinchen, TE, LSU.

Minnesota Vikings

19. Randall McDaniel, G, Arizona St.; 54. Brad Edwards, DB, So. Carolina; 71. Al Noga, DE, Hawaii; 108, Todd Kalis, G, Arizona St.; 124. Darrell Fullington, DB, Miami; 154. Derrick White, DB, Oklahoma; 183. Brad Beckman, TE, Nebraska-Omaha; 210. Joe Cain, LB, Oregon Tech; 237. Paul McGowan, LB, Florida St.; 264. Brian Habib, DT, Washington; 296. Norman Floyd, DB, So. Carolina.

New England Patriots

17. John Stephens, RB, Northwest (LA) St.; 43. Vincent Brown, LB, Miss. Valley St.; 69. Tom Rehder, T, Notre Dame; 87. Tim Goad, DT, No. Carolina; 97. Sammy Martin, WR, LSU; 100. Teddy Garcia, K, Northeast Louisiana; 115. Troy Wolkow, G, Minnesota; 154. Steve Johnson, TE, Virginia Tech; 181. Darryl Usher, WR, Illinois; 240. Neil Galbraith, DB, Central St. (OK); 267. Rodney Lossow, C, Wisconsin; 294. Marvin Allen, RB, Tulane; 321. Dave Nugent, DT, Boston College.

New Orleans Saints

24. Craig Heyward, RB, Pitt; 52. Brett Perriman, WR, Miami; 81. Tony Stephens, DT, Clemson; 106. Lydell Carr, RB, Oklahoma; 112. Greg Scales, TE, Wake Forest; 134. Keith Taylor, DB, Illinois; 162. Bob Sims, G, Florida; 190. Brian Forde, LB, Washington St.; 218. Glenn Derby, T, Wisconsin; 246. Clarence Nunn, DB, San Diego St.; 274. Todd Santos, QB, San Diego St.; 276. Vincent Fizer, LB, Southern; 302. Gary Couch, WR, Minnesota; 330. Paul Jurgensen, DE, Georgia Tech.

New York Giants

10. Eric Moore, T, Indiana; 36. John Elliott, T, Michigan; 62. Sheldon White, DB, Miami (Ohio); 92. Ricky Shaw, LB, Oklahoma St.; 118. Jon Carter, DE, Pitt; 145. David Houle, G, Michigan St.; 175. Mike Perez, QB, San Jose St.; 186. Danta Whitaker, TE, Mississippi Valley St.; 202. Sammy Lilly, DB, Georgia Tech; 259. Eric Hickerson, DB, Indiana; 265. Steve Wilkes, TE, Appalachian St.; 286. Greg Harris, WR, Troy St.; 313. David Futrell, DT, Brigham Young; 323. Brendan McCormick, DT, So. Carolina.

New York Jets

8. David Cadigan, T, So. California; 37. Terry Williams, DB, Bethune-Cookman; 63. Erik McMillan, DB, Missouri; 74. James Hasty, DB, Washington St.; 119. Mike Withycombe, T, Fresno St.; 146. Paul Frase, DT, Syracuse; 173. Gary Patton, RB, E. Michigan; 203. Keith Neubert, TE, Nebraska; 230. Ralph Tamm, G, West Chester (PA); 257. John Booty, DB, TCU; 287. John Galvin, LB, Boston Col.; 314. Albert Goss, DT, Jackson St.

Philadelphia Eagles

13. Keith Jackson, TE, Oklahoma; 30. Eric Allen, DB, Arizona St.; 65. Matt Patchan, T, Miami; 122, Eric Everett, DB, Texas Tech; 149. Don McPherson, QB, Syracuse; 160. Rob Sterling, DB, Maine; 176. Todd White, WR, Cal. St.-Fullerton; 207. David Smith, RB, W. Kentucky; 261. Joe Schuster, DT, Iowa; 288. Izel Jenkins, DB, No. Carolina St.; 319. Steve Kaufusi, DE, Brigham Young.

Phoenix Cardinals

12. Ken Harvey, LB, California; 38. Tony Jeffery, RB, TCU; 68. Tom Tupa, QB/P, Ohio St.; 95. Michael Brim, DB, Virginia Union; 120. Chris Gaines, LB, Vanderbilt; 132. Tony Jordan, RB, Kansas St.; 148. Jon Phillips, G, Oklahoma; 179. Ernie Jones, WR, Indiana; 206. Tim Moore, LB, Michigan St.; 233. Scott Dill, G, Memphis St.; 260. Andy Schillinger, WR, Miami (OH); 291. Keith McCoy, DB, Fresno St.; 318. Chris Carrier, DB, LSU.

Pittsburgh Steelers

18. Aaron Jones, DE, E. Kentucky; 44. Dermontti Dawson, G, Kentucky; 70. Chuck Lanza, C, Notre Dame; 121. Darin Jordan, LB, Northeastern; 128. Jerry Reese, DT, Kentucky; 155. Warren Williams, RB, Miami; 182. Marc Zeno, WR, Tulane; 209. Mark Nichols, DT, Michigan St.; 211. Mike Hinnant, TE, Temple; 236. Gordie Lickbaum, RB, Holy Cross; 252. John Jackson, T, E. Kentucky; 295. Bobby Dawson, DB, Illinois; 322. James Earle, LB, Clemson.

San Diego Chargers

15. Anthony Miller, WR, Tennessee; 60. Quinn Early, WR, Iowa; 91. Joe Campbell, DE, New Mexico St.; 93. Stacey Searels, T, Auburn; 98. Dave Richards, T, UCLA; 152. Cedric Figaro, LB, Notre Dame; 238. Joey Howard, T, Tennessee; 285. Ed Miller, C, Pitt; 292. George Hinkle, DT, Arizona; 324. Wendell Phillips, DB, Northern Alabama.

San Francisco 49ers

33. Daniel Stubbs, DE, Miami; 39. Pierce Holt, DT, Angelo St.; 80. Bill Romanowski, LB, Boston Col.; 103. Barry Helton, P, Colorado; 191. Kevin Bryant, LB, Delaware St.; 219. Larry Clarkson, T, Montana; 247. Brian Bonner, LB, Minnesota; 275. Tim Foley, K, Georgia Southern; 303. Terrance Brooks, DB, Texas A&M; 331. George Mira, LB, Miami.

Seattle Seahawks

49. Brian Blades, WR, Miami; 75. Tommy Kane, WR, Syracuse; 101. Kevin Harmon, RB, Iowa; 158. Roy Hart, DT, So. Carolina; 185. Ray Jackson, DB, Ohio St.; 215. Robert Tyler, TE, So. Carolina St.; 242. Deatrick Wise, DT, Jackson St.; 269. Derwin Jones, DT, Miami; 284. Rick McLeod, T, Washington; 299. Dwayne Harper, DB, So. Carolina St.; 326. Dave DesRochers, T, San Diego St.

Tampa Bay Buccaneers

4. Paul Gruber, T, Wisconsin; 53. Lars Tate, RB, Georgia; 83. Robert Goff, DT, Auburn; 86. John Bruhn, G, Tennessee; 107. Monte Robbins, P, Michigan; 113. William Howard, RB, Tennessee; 163. Shawn Lee, DT, Northern Alabama; 167. Kerry Goode, RB, Alabama; 198. Anthony Simpson, RB, E. Carolina; 225. Reuben Davis, DT, No. Carolina; 279. Frank Pillow, WR, Tennessee St.; 310. Victor Jones, LB, Virginia Tech.

Washington Redskins

55. Chip Lohmiller, K, Minnesota; 64. Mike Oliphant, RB, Puget Sound; 109. Jamie Morris, RB, Michigan; 127. Carl Mims, DB, Sam Houston St.; 159. Stan Humphries, QB, Northeast Louisiana; 193. Harold Hicks, DB, San Diego St.; 221. Darryl McGill, RB, Wake Forest; 249. Blake Peterson, LB, Mesa Col.; 277. Henry Brown, T, Ohio St.; 305. Curt Koch, DE, Colorado; 315. Wayne Ross, P, San Diego St.

1987
Statistics

Leading Rushers	Att.	Yards	Avg.	TDs
AFC				
Dickerson, Ind.	283	1288	4.6	6
Warner, Sea.	234	985	4.2	8
Rozier, Hou.	229	957	4.2	3
Allen, Raiders	200	754	3.8	5
Winder, Den.	196	741	3.8	6
Mack, Cle.	201	735	3.7	5
Jackson, Pitt.	180	696	3.9	1
Okoye, K.C.	157	660	4.2	3
Bentley, Ind.	142	631	4.4	7
Stradford, Mia.	145	619	4.3	6
Kinnebrew, Cin.	145	570	3.9	8
Jackson, Raiders	81	554	6.8	4
Pollard, Pitt.	128	536	4.2	3
McNeil, Jets	121	530	4.4	0
Williams, Sea.	113	500	4.4	1
Harmon, Buff.	116	485	4.2	2
Collins, N.E.	147	474	3.2	3
Heard, K.C.	82	466	5.7	3
Abercrombie, Pitt.	123	459	3.7	2
Hector, Jets	111	435	3.9	11
NFC				
White, Rams	324	1374	4.2	11
Mayes, N.O.	243	917	3.8	5

Leading Rushers	Att.	Yards	Avg.	TDs
Walker, Dall.	209	891	4.3	7
Riggs, Atl.	203	875	4.3	2
Craig, S.F.	215	815	3.8	3
Mitchell, St. L.	203	781	3.8	3
Morris, Giants	193	658	3.4	3
Nelson, Minn.	131	642	4.9	0
Rogers, Wash.	163	613	3.8	6
Anderson, Chi.	129	586	4.5	3
Payton, Chi.	146	533	3.7	4
Ferrell, St. L.	113	512	4.5	7
Hilliard, N.O.	123	508	4.1	7
Cunningham, Phil.	76	505	6.6	3
Wilder, T.B.	106	488	4.6	0
Toney, Phil.	127	473	3.7	5
Dorsett, Dall.	130	456	3.5	1
Byers, Phil.	116	426	3.7	3
Davis, G.B.	109	413	3.8	3
Bryant, Wash.	77	406	5.3	1

Leading Passers	Att.	Comp.	Yds. Gnd.	TD Pass	Int.	Rating
AFC						
Kosar, Cle.	389	241	3033	22	9	95.4
Marino, Mia.	444	263	3245	26	13	89.2
Krieg, Sea.	294	178	2131	23	15	87.6
Kenney, K.C.	273	154	2107	15	9	85.8
Wilson, Raiders	266	152	2070	12	8	84.6
Kelly, Buff.	419	250	2798	19	11	83.8
Elway, Den.	410	224	3198	19	12	83.4
O'Brien, Jets	393	234	2696	13	8	82.8
Trudeau, Ind.	229	128	1587	6	6	75.4
Moon, Hou.	368	184	2806	21	18	74.2
Esiason, Cin.	440	240	3321	16	19	73.1
Fouts, S.D.	364	206	2517	10	15	70.0
Malone, Pitt.	336	156	1896	6	19	46.7

Leading Passers	Att.	Comp.	Yds. Gnd.	TD Pass	Int.	Rat- ing
NFC						
Montana, S.F.	398	266	3054	31	13	102.1
Simms, Giants	282	163	2230	17	9	90.0
Lomax, St. L.	463	275	3387	24	12	88.5
McMahon, Chi.	210	125	1639	12	8	87.4
DeBerg, T.B.	275	159	1891	14	7	85.3
Cunningham, Phil.	406	223	2786	23	12	83.0
Hebert, N.O.	294	164	2119	15	9	82.9
Wilson, Minn.	264	140	2106	14	13	76.7
White, Dall.	362	215	2617	12	17	73.2
Schroeder, Wash.	267	129	1878	12	10	71.0
Everett, Rams	302	162	2064	10	13	68.4
Campbell, Atl.	260	136	1728	11	14	65.0
Long, Det.	417	232	2598	11	20	63.2
Wright, G.B.	247	132	1507	6	11	61.6

Leading Receivers	No.	Yards	Avg.	TDs
AFC				
Toon, Jets	68	976	14.4	5
Largent, Sea.	58	912	15.7	8
Reed, Buff.	57	752	13.2	5
Burkett, Buff.	56	765	13.7	4
Harmon, Buff.	56	477	8.5	2
Carson, K.C.	55	1044	19.0	7
Givins, Hou.	53	933	17.6	6
Winslow, S.D.	53	519	9.8	3
Byner, Cle.	52	552	10.6	2
Brooks, Ind.	51	722	14.2	3
Allen, Raiders	51	410	8.0	0
Hill, Hou.	49	989	20.2	6
Stradford, Mia.	48	457	9.5	1
Slaughter, Cle.	47	806	17.1	7
Christensen, Raiders	47	663	14.1	2
Anderson, S.D.	47	503	10.7	2
Clayton, Mia.	46	776	16.9	7

Leading Receivers	No.	Yards	Avg.	TDs
NFC				
Smith. St. L.	91	1117	12.3	8
Craig, S.F.	66	492	7.5	1
Rice, S.F.	65	1078	16.6	22
Walker, Dall.	60	715	11.9	1
Mandley, Det.	58	720	12.4	7
Clark, Wash.	56	1066	19.0	7
Bavaro, Giants	55	867	15.8	8
Ellard, Rams	51	799	15.7	3
Anderson, Chi.	47	467	9.9	3
Quick, Phil.	46	790	17.2	11
Renfro, Dall.	46	662	14.4	4
Mitchell, St. L.	45	397	8.8	2
Martin, N.O.	44	778	17.7	7
Green, St. L.	43	731	17.0	4
Bryant, Wash.	43	490	11.4	5
Awalt, St. L.	42	526	12.5	6

Leading Interceptors	No.	Yards	Long	TDs
AFC				
Prior, Ind.	6	57	38	0
Kelso, Buff.	6	25	12	0
Bostic, Hou.	6	−14	7	0
Woodruff, Pitt.	5	91	133	1
Smith, S.D.	5	28	12	0
NFC				
Wilburn, Wash.	9	135	100	1
Griffin, Det.	6	130	29	0
Browner, Minn.	6	67	23	0
Kinard, Giants	5	163	70	1
Waymer, N.O.	5	78	35	0
Sutton, N.O.	5	68	26	0
Curtis, St. L.	5	65	31	0
Lott, S.F.	5	62	34	0
Walls, Dall.	5	38	30	0
Griffin, S.F.	5	1	1	0

Leading Scorers, Kicking	PAT	FG	Long	TP
AFC				
Breech, Cin.	25/27	24/30	46	97
Biasucci, Ind.	24/24	24/27	50	96
Zendejas, Hou.	32/33	20/26	52	92
Karlis, Den.	37/37	18/25	51	91
Anderson, Pitt.	21/21	22/27	52	87
Johnson, Sea.	40/40	15/20	49	85
Leahy, Jets	31/31	18/22	42	85
Bahr, Raiders	27/28	19/29	48	84
NFC				
Andersen, N.O.	37/37	28/36	52	121
Ruzek, Dall.	26/26	22/25	49	92
Lansford, Rams	36/38	17/21	48	87
Butler, Chi.	28/30	19/28	52	85
McFadden, Phil.	36/36	16/26	49	84
Wersching, S.F.	44/46	13/17	45	83
Murray, Det.	21/21	20/32	53	81
Allegre, Giants	25/26	17/27	53	76

Leading Scorers, Touchdowns	TDs	Rush	Rec.	Ret.	TP
AFC					
Hector, Jets	11	11	0	0	66
Byner, Cle.	10	8	2	0	60
Warner, Sea.	10	8	2	0	60
Bentley, Ind.	9	7	2	0	54
Riddick, Buff.	8	5	3	0	50*
Duper, Mia.	8	0	8	0	48
Kinnebrew, Cin.	8	8	0	0	48
Largent, Sea.	8	0	8	0	48
Carson, K.C.	7	0	7	0	42
Clayton, Mia.	7	0	7	0	42
Johnson, Den.	7	0	7	0	42
Slaughter, Cle.	7	0	7	0	42
Stradford, Mia.	7	6	1	0	42
Winder, Den.	7	6	1	0	42

*Includes safety.

Leading Scorers, Touchdowns	TDs	Rush	Rec.	Ret.	TP
NFC					
Rice, S.F.	23	1	22	0	138
Quick, Phil.	11	0	11	0	66
White, Rams	11	11	0	0	66
Bavaro, Giants	8	0	8	0	48
Hilliard, N.O.	8	7	1	0	48
Smith, St. L.	8	0	8	0	48
Walker, Dall.	8	7	1	0	48
Carter, Minn.	7	0	7	0	42
Clark, Wash.	7	0	7	0	42
Dozier, Minn.	7	5	2	0	42
Ferrell, St. L.	7	7	0	0	42
Gault, Chi.	7	0	7	0	42
Mandley, Det.	7	0	7	0	42
Martin, N.O.	7	0	7	0	42

Leading Punters	No.	Yards	Long	Avg.
AFC				
Mojsiejenko, S.D.	67	2875	57	42.9
Newsome, Pitt.	64	2678	57	41.8
Fulhage, Cin.	52	2168	58	41.7
Horan, Den.	44	1807	61	41.1
Goodburn, K.C.	59	2412	55	40.9
Talley, Raiders	56	2277	63	40.7
Gossett, Hou.	44	1777	55	40.4
Camarillo, N.E.	62	2489	73	40.1
Rodriguez, Sea.	47	1880	63	40.0
Stark, Ind.	61	2440	63	40.0
Johnson, Cle.	50	1969	66	39.4
Kidd, Buff.	64	2495	67	39.0
Jennings, Jets	64	2444	58	38.2
NFC				
Donnelly, Atl.	61	2686	62	44.0
Arnold, Det.	46	2007	60	43.6
Landeta, Giants	65	2773	64	42.7
Hatcher, Rams	76	3140	62	41.3

Leading Punters	No.	Yards	Long	Avg.
Bracken, G.B.	72	2947	65	40.9
Cox, Wash.	63	2571	77	40.8
Hansen, N.O.	52	2104	60	40.5
Horne, St. L.	43	1730	57	40.2
Coleman, Minn.	45	1786	54	39.7
Saxon, Dall.	68	2685	63	39.5
Runager, S.F.	55	2157	56	39.2
Garcia, T.B.	62	2409	58	38.9
Teltschik, Phil.	82	3131	60	38.2
Cater, St. L.	39	1470	68	37.7

Leading Punt Returners	No.	Yards	Avg.	TDs
AFC				
Edmonds, Sea.	20	251	12.6	0
James, S.D.	32	400	12.5	1
Townsell, Jets	32	381	11.9	1
McNeil, Cle.	34	386	11.4	0
Martin, Cin.	28	277	9.9	0
Clemons, K.C.	19	162	8.5	0
Schwedes, Mia.	24	203	8.5	0
Johnson, Hou.	24	196	8.2	0
Woods, Raiders	26	189	7.3	0
Pitts, Buff.	23	149	6.5	0
NFC				
Gray, N.O.	24	352	14.7	0
McLemore, S.F.	21	265	12.6	1
Lewis, Minn.	22	275	12.5	1
Sikahema, St. L.	44	550	12.5	1
Mandley, Det.	23	250	10.9	0
McKinnon, Chi.	40	405	10.1	2
Martin, Dall.	22	216	9.8	0
McConkey, Giants	42	394	9.4	0
Futrell, T.B.	24	213	8.9	0
Johnson, Atl.	21	168	8.0	0

Leading Kickoff Returners	No.	Yards	Avg.	TDs
AFC				
Palmer, K.C.	38	923	24.3	2
Bentley, Ind.	22	500	22.7	0
Mueller, Raiders	27	588	21.8	0
Holland, S.D.	19	410	21.6	0
Edmonds, Sea.	27	564	20.9	0
Stone, Pitt.	28	568	20.3	0
Anderson, S.D.	22	433	19.7	0
Duncan, Hou.	28	546	19.5	0
Starring, N.E.	23	445	19.3	0
Bussey, Cin.	21	406	19.3	0
NFC				
Stamps, Atl.	24	660	27.5	1
Gentry, Chi.	25	621	24.8	1
Rouson, Giants	22	497	22.6	0
Lee, Det.	32	719	22.5	0
Guggemos, Minn.	36	808	22.4	0
Sikahema, St. L.	34	761	22.4	0
Clack, Dall.	29	635	21.9	0
Brown, Rams	27	581	21.5	1
Fullwood, G.B.	24	510	21.3	0
Gray, N.O.	30	636	21.2	0

1988
NFL Schedule

Sunday, September 4
Atlanta at Detroit
Dallas at Pittsburgh
L.A. Rams at Green Bay
Miami at Chicago
Minnesota at Buffalo
Philadelphia at Tampa Bay
Phoenix at Cincinnati
San Fran. at New Orleans
N.Y. Jets at New England
Houston at Indianapolis
San Diego at L.A. Raiders
Seattle at Denver
Cleveland at Kansas City

Monday, September 5
Washington at N.Y. Giants

Sunday, September 11
Chicago at Indianapolis
Miami at Buffalo
New Orleans at Atlanta
Pittsburgh at Washington
San Fran. at N.Y. Giants
Tampa Bay at Green Bay
San Diego at Denver
N.Y. Jets at Cleveland
New England at Minnesota
L.A. Raiders at Houston
Detroit at L.A. Rams
Kansas City at Seattle
Cincinnati at Phil.

Monday, September 12
Dallas at Phoenix

Sunday, September 18
Buffalo at New England
Cincinnati at Pittsburgh
Denver at Kansas City
Green Bay at Miami
Houston at N.Y. Jets
Minnesota at Chicago
New Orleans at Detroit
Phil. at Washington
Phoenix at Tampa Bay
Seattle at San Diego
N.Y. Giants at Dallas
L.A. Rams at L.A. Raiders
Atlanta at San Fran.

Monday, September 19
Indianapolis at Cleveland

Sunday, September 25
Atlanta at Dallas
Chicago at Green Bay
Cleveland at Cincinnati
Miami at Indianapolis
New England at Houston
N.Y. Jets at Detroit
Philadelphia at Minnesota
Pittsburgh at Buffalo
Tampa Bay at New Orl.
San Diego at Kansas City

San Fran. at Seattle
Washington at Phoenix
L.A. Rams at N.Y. Giants

Monday, September 26
L.A. Raiders at Denver

Sunday, October 2
Buffalo at Chicago
Cleveland at Pittsburgh
Green Bay at Tampa Bay
Houston at Philadelphia
Indianap. at New England
N.Y. Giants at Washington
Seattle at Atlanta
Phoenix at L.A. Rams
Kansas City at N.Y. Jets
Cincinnati at L.A. Raiders
Denver at San Diego
Detroit at San Francisco
Minnesota at Miami

Monday, October 3
Dallas at New Orleans

Sunday, October 9
Chicago at Detroit
Indianapolis at Buffalo
Kansas City at Houston
L.A. Rams at Atlanta
New England vs. Green Bay
   at Milwaukee
N.Y. Jets at Cincinnati
Seattle at Cleveland
Tampa Bay at Minnesota
Washington at Dallas
Pittsburgh at Phoenix
Denver at San Francisco
Miami at L.A. Raiders
New Orleans at San Diego

Monday, October 10
N.Y. Giants at Phil.

Sunday, October 16
Cincinnati at New England
Dallas at Chicago
Detroit at N.Y. Giants
Green Bay at Minnesota
Houston at Pittsburgh
L.A. Raiders at Kan. City
Philadelphia at Cleveland
Phoenix at Washington
San Diego at Miami
Tampa Bay at Indianapolis
San Fran. at L.A. Rams
New Orleans at Seattle
Atlanta at Denver

Monday, October 17
Buffalo at N.Y. Jets

Sunday, October 23
Dallas at Philadelphia
Denver at Pittsburgh
Detroit at Kansas City
Houston at Cincinnati
L.A. Raiders at New Orl.
Minnesota at Tampa Bay
New England at Buffalo
Washington vs. Green Bay
   at Milwaukee
N.Y. Giants at Atlanta
N.Y. Jets at Miami
Seattle at L.A. Rams
Indianapolis at San Diego
Cleveland at Phoenix

Monday, October 24
San Francisco at Chicago

Sunday, October 30
Atlanta at Philadelphia

Chicago at New England
Cincinnati at Cleveland
Green Bay at Buffalo
L.A. Rams at New Orleans
Miami at Tampa Bay
N.Y. Giants at Detroit
Phoenix at Dallas
Pittsburgh at N.Y. Jets
San Diego at Seattle
Minnesota at San Fran.
Kan. City at L.A. Raiders
Washington at Houston

Monday, October 31
Denver at Indianapolis

Sunday, November 6
Dallas at N.Y. Giants
Detroit at Minnesota
Green Bay at Atlanta
L.A. Rams at Phil.
Miami at New England
Pittsburgh at Cincinnati
Tampa Bay at Chicago
San Francisco at Phoenix
N.Y. Jets at Indianap.
New Orl. at Washington
Kansas City at Denver
Buffalo at Seattle
L.A. Raiders at San Diego

Monday, November 7
Cleveland at Houston

Sunday, November 13
Chicago at Washington
Cincinnati at Kansas City
Indianapolis at Green Bay
New England at N.Y. Jets
Phil. at Pittsburgh
San Diego at Atlanta
Tampa Bay at Detroit

L.A. Raiders at San Fran.
New Orleans at L.A. Rams
N.Y. Giants at Phoenix
Cleveland at Denver
Houston at Seattle
Minnesota at Dallas

Monday, November 14
Buffalo at Miami

Sunday, November 20
Chicago at Tampa Bay
Cincinnati at Dallas
Denver at New Orleans
Detroit vs. Green Bay
   at Milwaukee
Indianapolis at Minnesota
N.Y. Jets at Buffalo
Phoenix at Houston
Pittsburgh at Cleveland
Seattle at Kansas City
San Diego at L.A. Rams
Phil. at N.Y. Giants
Atlanta at L.A. Raiders
New England at Miami

Monday, November 21
Washington at San Fran.

Thursday, November 24
Minnesota at Detroit
Houston at Dallas

Sunday, November 27
Buffalo at Cincinnati
Cleveland at Washington
Green Bay at Chicago
Kansas City at Pittsburgh
Miami at N.Y. Jets
Phoenix at Philadelphia
Tampa Bay at Atlanta
San Fran. at San Diego

New England at Indianap.
L.A. Rams at Denver
N.Y. Giants at New Orl.

Monday, November 28
L.A. Raiders at Seattle

Sunday, December 4
Buffalo at Tampa Bay
Dallas at Cleveland
Green Bay at Detroit
Indianapolis at Miami
New Orleans at Minnesota
Phoenix at N.Y. Giants
San Diego at Cincinnati
San Fran. at Atlanta
Seattle at New England
Washington at Phil.
N.Y. Jets at Kansas City
Denver at L.A. Raiders
Pittsburgh at Houston

Monday, December 5
Chicago at L.A. Rams

Saturday, December 10
Indianap. at N.Y. Jets
Philadelphia at Phoenix

Sunday, December 11
Cincinnati at Houston
Dallas at Washington

Detroit at Chicago
Kan. City at N.Y. Giants
Tampa Bay at New Eng.
L.A. Raiders at Buffalo
Minnesota at Green Bay
New Orleans at San Fran.
Pittsburgh at San Diego
Atlanta at L.A. Rams
Denver at Seattle

Monday, December 12
Cleveland at Miami

Saturday, December 17
Washington at Cincinnati
New England at Denver

Sunday, December 18
Atlanta at New Orleans
Buffalo at Indianapolis
Detroit at Tampa Bay
Houston at Cleveland
Miami at Pittsburgh
N.Y. Giants at N.Y. Jets
Philadelphia at Dallas
Seattle at L.A. Raiders
Kansas City at San Diego
Green Bay at Phoenix
L.A. Rams at San Fran.

Monday, December 19
Chicago at Minnesota

BRUCE WEBER PICKS
HOW THEY'LL FINISH IN 1988

AFC East

1. New England
2. Indianapolis
3. Buffalo
4. Miami
5. N.Y. Jets

AFC Central

1. Cleveland
2. Pittsburgh
3. Cincinnati
4. Houston

AFC West

1. Seattle
2. Denver
3. L.A. Raiders
4. San Diego
5. Kansas City

NFC East

1. N.Y. Giants
2. Washington
3. Philadelphia
4. Dallas
5. Phoenix

NFC Central

1. Chicago
2. Minnesota
3. Tampa Bay
4. Green Bay
5. Detroit

NFC West

1. New Orleans
2. San Francisco
3. L.A. Rams
4. Atlanta

AFC Champions: Cleveland
NFC Champions: N.Y. Giants
Super Bowl Champions: N.Y. Giants

YOU PICK
HOW THEY'LL FINISH IN 1988

AFC East

1.
2.
3.
4.
5.

AFC Central

1.
2.
3.
4.

AFC West

1.
2.
3.
4.
5.

NFC East

1.
2.
3.
4.
5.

NFC Central

1.
2.
3.
4.
5.

NFC West

1.
2.
3.
4.

AFC Champions:
NFC Champions:
Super Bowl Champions: